GOD I'M RETURNING YOUR WORD IT DON'T WORK

GOD I'M RETURNING YOUR WORD IT DON'T WORK

HOW TO WORK THE WORD

PASTOR TYRONE JOHNSON

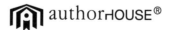

AuthorHouse™ LLC
1663 Liberty Drive
Bloomington, IN 47403
www.authorhouse.com
Phone: 1-800-839-8640

Published by AuthorHouse 02/25/2014

ISBN: 978-1-4918-6619-1 (sc)
ISBN: 978-1-4918-6620-7 (hc)
ISBN: 978-1-4918-6621-4 (e)

Library of Congress Control Number: 2014903256

Scripture quotations marked KJV are from the Holy Bible, King James Version (Authorized Version). First published in 1611. Quoted from the KJV Classic Reference Bible, Copyright © 1983 by The Zondervan Corporation.

CONTENTS

INTRODUCTION

Have you ever spoken the Word of God over your life or someone else's life and then watched God work? Then other times you've spoken the Word and nothing happened. What would you do if you brought a product from the store and sometimes it worked and sometimes it didn't work? You would more than likely return it to the store and complain about it. This book is designed to teach the reader about the Word of God and how the Word work. The reader will also learn how to use the Word of God more effectively in their life and the lives of others.

To gain an understanding of how the Words of God works we must first have some understanding of spiritual laws. Most people do not understand the operation of spiritual laws. We do not have a problem with physical laws; we have learned to obey and respect them. We know that if we step off of a building, we are going to hit the ground. It doesn't matter who we are or even how long we prayed that morning, we are going down. Spiritual laws, too, are real and they are mostly operated by words. This book teaches of the authority of God's Word, and why God's Word always comes to pass. The reader will also learn why God's Word must be spoken by men in the earth in order to bring things to pass. The readers will not only learn about God's Word, they will also learn the power of their own words and how to use them effectively.

Finally, We will look into the Word of God and see how the bible uses every day things that we do to help us understand how the word of God works, for example: *Heb. Chapter 4* God's Word is compared to a sword, *John Chapter 4* God's Word is compared to a well of living water, *Am. Chapter 7* God's Word is compared to a plumb line, *Mk Chapter 4* God's word is like a seed, *Jer. 23* God's Word is like fire, *Isa. 55:9* God's Word is like the rain. I believe the better we understand how the Word works, the more skilled we will become in using the Word, and the more effective we will be at changing our lives and helping to change the lives of others.

CHAPTER I

IN THE BEGINNING

John 1:1-2 In the beginning was the Word, and the Word was with God, and the Word was God. 2 The same was in the beginning with God.

Gen 1:1 In the beginning God created the Heaven and the earth.

John tells us in John 1:1-2 In *the beginning was the Word*, but Genesis 1:1 said '*in the beginning, God,*' so which is it? The answer is both. God gives us the answer in verse 2 of John chapter 1:2: *the same was in the beginning with God.* We cannot separate God from His Word; God and His Word are the same. Or you could say that God is as good as His Word. We as Christians should strive to be as good as our word. Most of us don't realize the importance of our words, and because of that, we don't think much about what we say. Because we do not value our own words, in return we do not value the words of others. If we are to be honest with ourselves, we don't really expect people to tell us the truth, we look for people to lie to us. Where do we get this mentality from? We get that mentality from ourselves. As we study the bible we find that God is big on words, words that He speaks and words that we speak. God not only expects us to honor

His Word, but He also expects us to honor our own words and the words of others that do not conflict with His Word.

One of the main things that make the Word of God powerful is that it was in the beginning. God's Word established who He was and is from the beginning. The Word of God is supreme and it is to be honored above all. The Word of God is honored and obeyed by Him. God honors His Word so much that God Himself is bound by His own Word. Likewise, God expects us to honor our word, and be bound by our word. The bible teaches us in:

Ps 15:4 *In whose eyes a vile person is contemned; but he honoureth them that fear the Lord. He that sweareth to his own hurt, and changeth not.*

We must remember that when we give our word to someone, we shouldn't change it. Even if it hurts us, we should stand by our words.

I remember from my childhood the saying, "Sticks and stone may break my bones, but words will never hurt me." As I grew up I found that to be very untrue. With our words we have the ability to make people happy or make people sad. With our words we can bless or curse. We can even touch people's emotions with our words. Most of us don't give much thought to the words we speak, because we don't fully understand the power of words. Because words are so powerful, when spoken they dictate how our life will go, and also plays a great part in our destiny. The Bible teaches us in James 3 that words set the course that our life will take:

James 3:3-6 *Behold, we put bits in the horses' mouths, that they may obey us; and we turn about their whole body.4 Behold also the ships, which though* *they be so great, and are driven of fierce winds, yet are they turned about with a very small helm, whithersoever the governor listeth.*

5 Even so the tongue is a little member, and boasteth great things. Behold, how great a matter a little fire kindleth!6 And the tongue is a fire, a world of iniquity: so is the tongue among our members, that it defileth the whole body, and setteth on fire the course of nature; and it is set on fire of hell.

One of the first things we learn as Christians is that God is faithful to His Word. Just like God's words establish who He is, our words should establish who we are. Have you ever met someone that didn't keep their word and didn't do what they said they would do? If so, this failure to keep their word probably established in your mind the type of person they were. When you deal with people that don't keep their word, it creates problems for you and prevents you from functioning at your best. Words are how we express ourselves to the people around us. Words also reveal things about us, whether good and bad. How we us words will tell people things about us that we may not want them to know. Words are our most valuable asset, but they can also be our worst enemy. The Bible teaches us that our words contain blessings and curses, life and death

James 3:10 *Out of the same mouth proceedeth blessing and cursing . . . .*

Prov 18:20-21 *A man's belly shall be satisfied with the fruit of his mouth; and with the increase of his lips shall he be filled. 21 Death and life are in the power of the tongue: and they that love it shall eat the fruit thereof.*

Our words alone carry power, but when we add faith to our words, our expectation rises. Even when we speak God's words, we must mix faith with them. Everything that we get out of God's Word will be based on whether or not we believe it and to what extent we believe it.

Heb 4:2 *For unto us was the gospel preached, as well as unto them: but the word preached did not profit them, not being mixed with faith in them that heard it.*

What we say is very important. For this reason, we must study the Word of God and learn the mind of God, so we can say what God said. We should always choose our words very carefully. Jesus taught us that we would have to give an account for the words that we spoke:

Matt 12:36 *But I say unto you, That every idle word that men shall speak, they shall give account thereof in the day of judgment.*

What is an idle word? An idle word is a word that is barren, inactive, unemployed, and useless: in other words, it is a word that doesn't do anyone any good. Notice that an idle word does not have to be a lie; it can be true and still be an idle word. Jesus is speaking here about the heart. In essence, what Jesus is saying is that any word we say with our mouths that does not agree with or come from our heart is an idle word. Can you imagine how many fewer words we would speak if we only spoke words that were useful and that came from the heart? A good habit to get into when you are not sure about what to say is to ask yourself the question, "Is what I am about to say going to do anybody any good, and is it coming from my heart?" If your answer is no to this question, then don't say it.

If you were to take inventory of your life, you would find that words played a large part in whatever position you are in now. Are you happy with your life? The right words spoken at the right time made that possible. Are you unhappy with your life? The wrong words spoken at the wrong time made that possible. Words should be very important to us as they are important to God. The reason words are so important is not only because they set the course of our future, but they also reveal our past. They can also reveal what's presently in your heart.

Have you ever heard the phrase "the art of listening"? Learning to listen is a good thing, but we must also learn to listen to ourselves, because we could learn a lot. Look at what Jesus said in Matt. 12:34:

Matt 12:34 *O generation of vipers, how can ye, being evil, speak good things? for out of the abundance of the heart the mouth speaketh.*

You would think that Jesus would have said "how can you, being evil, do good things". But Jesus said "speak" because Jesus knew that what we speak is what we get.

As Christians we often use the term "THE WORD OF GOD", but what are we really saying? Are we saying that God uses different words than us? Of course not, we are using the same words God has already spoken. Then why do God's words work for Him and not for us? Because we are not following the instructions we were given about using the words; we are not mixing them with faith. If you were to study the New Testament you would see the terms "Kingdom of God" or "Kingdom of heaven." These terms identify God's kingdom. We cannot fully see God's kingdom now, but in the future it will be fully manifested. The bible teaches us that the kingdom of God is within us, and we are to live our lives from within. Just as words affect our earthly life, words also affect how we function in the kingdom of God. God created both kingdoms—the earthly kingdom and the kingdom of God—to function by words. God gave us a perfect example of how words work in *John 1:14:*

John 1:14 And the Word was made flesh, and dwelt among us, (and we beheld his glory, the glory as of the only begotten of the Father,) full of grace and truth.

God spoke the Word in the beginning and the Word became flesh. The main thing we learn from this is that when we speak, the words that we speak have the ability to become what we speak. The reason we speak the words of God is because God has already spoken those words and He have spoken them with faith, and God's faith in His Word are what brings His Words to pass. Because God has spoken His words with faith, we can expect God's words to come to pass. Whenever we speak God's Word, we must also speak them with the faith of God.

One might ask, if God has already spoken the words, why do I need to speak them again? That is a very good question, and the answer is because man has dominion on this earth, and God's Word must be spoken in the earth in order for God's kingdom to be manifested in the earth.

Gen 1:26 And God said, Let us make man in our image, after our likeness: and let them have dominion over the fish of the sea, and over the fowl of the air, and over the cattle, and over all the earth, and over every creeping thing that creepeth upon the earth.

The first thing we learn is that to have dominion you must be a man or woman. God gave man dominion in the earth, so what man speaks in the earth carries authority in the earth.

John 4:24 *God is a Spirit: and they that worship him must worship him in spirit and in truth.*

If we want God's will done in the earth, we must speak God's words in the earth. This is why God gave us His Word, not just to live by, but also to speak it in the earth. God spoke in the garden, after man's sin, that He would send a seed through the women that would defeat Satan.

Gen 3:15 *And I will put enmity between thee and the woman, and between thy seed and her seed; it shall bruise thy head, and thou shalt bruise his heel.*

Although God had already spoken these words, man had to speak them again in the earth because man has the dominion. God used a number of prophets to speak in the earth about His plan to save man. To name just a few:

Ps 112:2 *His seed shall be mighty upon earth: the generation of the upright shall be blessed.*

Isa 7:14 *Therefore the Lord himself shall give you a sign; Behold, a virgin shall conceive, and bear a son, and shall call his name Immanuel.*

Isa 59:20 *And the Redeemer shall come to Zion, and unto them that turn from transgression in Jacob, saith the Lord.*

Can you imagine what Isaiah must have thought after he said, "Behold a virgin shall conceive"? Isaiah must have thought, "Man, what did I just say? A virgin can't have a baby." But Isaiah was speaking through the spirit of God.

It would be very helpful for us to remember that God is a spirit and not a man. Because of this, God must work in the earth through man, because man has the dominion. If God did not allow man to have dominion, then He would be in violation of His own Word. As Christians our main focus should be to bring God's Kingdom to the earth by allowing God to live through us.

The world will not be able to see God's Kingdom, but they will be able to see the effects of God's Kingdom through us. This is what Jesus meant when He spoke to Nicodemus in John 3:

John 3:3 *Jesus answered and said unto him, Verily, verily, I say unto thee, Except a man be born again, he cannot see the kingdom of God.*

We cannot expect the world to see God's kingdom because they haven't been born again. But we as Christians walk in the principles of God's kingdom, we can manifest the effects of the kingdom in the earth, thereby allowing the world to see the effects of God's kingdom. Jesus used the wind as an example of how the effects of the kingdom can be seen.

John 3:8 *The wind bloweth where it listeth, and thou hearest the sound thereof, but canst not tell whence it cometh, and whither it goeth: . . .*

You have probably used the expression "look at that wind," but in reality we can't see the wind. Rather, what we really see are the effects of the wind, and because of the effects, we know that the wind is present. The Kingdom of God works the same way. The world may not see the kingdom, but because of the effects in our lives, the world should know that the Kingdom is present.

As we begin to learn how to work the Word, we must also learn about the kingdom of God. The reason the kingdom of God will be the major factor in learning to work the Word is because everything in God's kingdom respond to God's Word. We must not have the mindset that says, "I will believe it when it see it." The bible teaches us that our walk with God is a faith walk.

Heb 11:6 *But without faith it is impossible to please him: for he that cometh to God must believe that he is, and that he is a rewarder of them that diligently seek him.*

2 Cor 5:7 *For we walk by faith, not by sight*

Rom 1:17 *. . . , The just shall live by faith.*

Faith is probably one of the most important topics in the bible. The reason Faith is so important is because if we are to live right, we must first believe right. What we believe is going to determine how we think and what we do. The bible teaches us in:

Prov 23:7 *For as he thinketh in his heart, so is he . . . .*

To be effective in God's kingdom we must understand God's purpose and remember that God's purpose is the only thing that counts. Not only do I need to understand God's purpose, I must also understand the role I play in God's purpose. My purpose in the earth is to show forth the glory of God. God's desire is to live in the earth through us, so He can show His goodness to the world through us. We MUST understand that everything that God does in the earth He will do through man.

As we begin to learn how to work the Word, we must believe that the Word is working in God's kingdom as we speak it. As God's Word works in His kingdom we will be able to see the effects in the earth, just like the wind.

Chapter I Scriptures

John 1:1-2 *In the beginning was the Word, and the Word was with God, and the Word was God.*

2 The same was in the beginning with God.

Gen 1:1 *In the beginning God created the Heaven and the earth.*

Ps 15:4 *In whose eyes a vile person is contemned; but he honoureth them that fear the Lord. He that sweareth to his own hurt, and changeth not.*

James 3:3-6 *Behold, we put bits in the horses' mouths, that they may obey us; and we turn about their whole body.4 Behold also the ships, which though they be so great, and are driven of fierce winds, yet are they turned about with a very small helm, whithersoever the governor listeth.5 Even so the tongue is a little member, and boasteth great things. Behold, how great a matter a little fire kindleth!*

6 And the tongue is a fire, a world of iniquity: so is the tongue among our members, that it defileth the whole body, and setteth on fire the course of nature; and it is set on fire of hell.

James 3:10 *Out of the same mouth proceedeth blessing and cursing. My brethren, these things ought not so to be.*

Prov 18:20-21 *20 A man's belly shall be satisfied with the fruit of his mouth; and with the increase of his lips shall he be filled.21 Death and life are in the power of the tongue: and they that love it shall eat the fruit thereof.*

Heb 4:2 *For unto us was the gospel preached, as well as unto them: but the word preached did not profit them, not being mixed with faith in them that heard it.*

Matt 12:36 *But I say unto you, That every idle word that men shall speak, they shall give account thereof in the day of judgment.*

Matt 12:34 *O generation of vipers, how can ye, being evil, speak good things? for out of the abundance of the heart the mouth speaketh.*

John 1:14 *And the Word was made flesh, and dwelt among us, (and we beheld his glory, the glory as of the only begotten of the Father,) full of grace and truth*

Gen 1:26 *And God said, Let us make man in our image, after our likeness: and let them have dominion over the fish of the sea, and over the fowl of the air, and over the cattle, and over all the earth, and over every creeping thing that creepeth upon the earth*

John 4:24 *God is a Spirit: and they that worship him must worship him in spirit and in truth.*

Gen 3:15 *And I will put enmity between thee and the woman, and between thy seed and her seed; it shall bruise thy head, and thou shalt bruise his heel*

Ps 112:2 *His seed shall be mighty upon earth: the generation of the upright shall be blessed.*

Isa 7:14 *Therefore the Lord himself shall give you a sign; Behold, a virgin shall conceive, and bear a son, and shall call his name Immanuel.*

Isa 59:20 *And the Redeemer shall come to Zion, and unto them that turn from transgression in Jacob, saith the Lord.*

John 3:3 *Jesus answered and said unto him, Verily, verily, I say unto thee, Except a man be born again, he cannot see the kingdom of God.*

John 3:8 *The wind bloweth where it listeth, and thou hearest the sound thereof, but canst not tell whence it cometh, and whither it goeth: so is every one that is born of the Spirit.*

Heb 11:6 *But without faith it is impossible to please him: for he that cometh to God must believe that he is, and that he is a rewarder of them that diligently seek him.*

2 Cor 5:7 *(For we walk by faith, not by sight:)*

Rom 1:17 *For therein is the righteousness of God revealed from faith to faith: as it is written, The just shall live by faith.*

Prov 23:7 *For as he thinketh in his heart, so is he: Eat and drink, saith he to thee; but his heart is not with thee.*

CHAPTER II

GOD HAS SPOKEN AND THAT SETTLES IT

The authority of the Word of God

If you grew up in a home where your parents constantly said that they were going to punish you when you misbehaved, but they never did, you soon learned not to take those words seriously and those words had no authority with you. Even as adults, if someone consistently tells us untruths, we don't trust or believe what they say. So where does authority come from? The Christian answer to this question would be that authority comes from God. Look what the bible teaches us in Rom. 13:1:

Rom 13:1 *Let every soul be subject unto the higher powers. For there is no power but of God: the powers that be are ordained of God.*

God's authority is not just because the bible said it: God's authority is because He is the creator of everything and it all belongs to Him. He is LORD of all.

Gen 1:1 *In the beginning God created the Heaven and the earth.*

Because God created the heavens and the earth, His Word carries authority there. Since God has all power and authority, He is the only one that can truly delegate authority to others.

As we look around in the world, it may seem like God's people are fighting a losing battle, but don't fear: God's Word still rules. Satan has fought the Word of God from the beginning, starting in the garden. Since then, Satan has fought to keep people away from the Word of God. He has fought to keep the Word of God out of our schools and our workplaces, and he has even fought to keep the Word of God out of our churches. Why is Satan so terrified by the Word of God? Satan is terrified by the Word of God because the Word of God has authority and power.

What is it that really gives words authority? The authority of words comes from the authority of the person who has spoken them. Do you remember the tale of the boy who cried wolf? The boy in that story had lied so much that his words had no power or authority, and in the end, no one listened to him. Satan's desire is to destroy God's people and one way that Satan tries to do this is by destroying the Christians' credibility with God and man. This is why Satan is called the accuser of the brethren in Rev. 12:10:

Rev 12:10 . . . . : *for the accuser of our brethren is cast down, which accused them before our God day and night.*

Have you ever noticed that in court, if a lawyer comes up against a witness that has damaging testimony against his client, he will challenge the credibility of that witness? The lawyer knows that if he can get the jury to question the credibility or the character of the witness, then they will also question what he says, even if the witness is telling the truth. Satan uses the same technique on the people of God; this is why Satan is constantly accusing the children of God. Satan knows that if our character is in question, then what we say will be less effective, even if we are speaking the Word of God.

To operate in the Word of God with authority only requires the answer to one simple question: do I believe what the Word of God says or not? It is not surprising that Christians do not understand the authority of the Word. Jesus Himself marveled when he saw that the centurion solder understood what it meant to have authority:

Matt 8:5-10 And when Jesus was entered into Capernaum, there came unto him a centurion, beseeching him, 6 And saying, Lord, my servant lieth at home sick of the palsy, grievously tormented. 7 And Jesus saith unto him, I will come and heal him. 8 The centurion answered and said, Lord, I am not worthy that thou shouldest come under my roof: but speak the word only, and my servant shall be healed. 9 For I am a man under authority, having soldiers under me: and I say to this man, Go, and he goeth; and to another, Come, and he cometh; and to my servant, Do this, and he doeth it. 10 When Jesus heard it, he marvelled, and said to them that followed, Verily I say unto you, I have not found so great faith, no, not in Israel.

This solder was not a man of God and didn't claim to be. This man was a Roman soldier, and being a Roman soldier he understood authority and how it worked. The centurion had some authority in the physical realm, but he had no authority in the spirit realm. The centurion knew that if he, being a Roman, had authority in the physical realm, then Jesus, being the

Christ, must have authority in the spirit realm. The Word of God carries authority in the spirit realm, as well as the physical realm. Let's look at how Jesus utilized His authority to cast out demons and at the same time is recognized in the physical realm:

Luke 4:35-36 *And Jesus rebuked him, saying, Hold thy peace, and come out of him. And when the devil had thrown him in the midst, he came out of him, and hurt him not.36 And they were all amazed, and spake among themselves, saying, What a word is this! for with authority and power he commandeth the unclean spirits, and they come out.*

Using the authority of the Word of God doesn't require that we be powerful, just that we have faith. One might ask the question, "Do I put my faith in the Word?" No, not just the Word, but always put your faith in God.

Mark 11:22 *And Jesus answering saith unto them, Have faith in God.*

When we have faith in God, then we will have faith in what God said. This is how we use the power and authority of the Word. We must understand who said it, and if God said it, it's already powerful because God is our King.

Eccl 8:4 *Where the word of a king is, there is power: and who may say unto him, What doest thou?*

Faith in the Word of God

Rom 10:17 *So then faith cometh by hearing, and hearing by the word of God.*

If we are going to operate in the power of the Word, we must have faith in the Word. Having faith in the Word is just like having faith in God.

John 1:1 *In the beginning was the Word, and the Word was with God, and the Word was God.*

How do I know when I have faith in the Word, and where do I get faith from? The bible teaches us that faith cometh by hearing. This sounds very theological, but what it means is whatever I continually hear is what I will begin to believe. This is a very important biblical principle which can work for us or against us. Whatever we believe about ourselves and our surroundings we came to believe it because we heard it. By understanding this principle, we can literally change what we believe by changing what we expose ourselves to. Notice also that this scripture says faith cometh by hearing, not by having heard. This means that we must continue to hear until we begin to believe. No one can say truthfully that they do not have any faith, because God has given everybody faith. Every person is born with the ability to hear and believe. Even if someone is born deaf and cannot hear sounds, however they communicate is how they hear. Hearing is not only physical, it is also spiritual.

Rom 12:3 *. . . , according as God hath dealt to every man the measure of faith.*

Hope in the Word

Before we can even begin to have faith in the Word, we must have hope in the Word. We will never successfully be able to believe that the Word will change our lives if we have no desire or hope that our lives will change. We often confuse hope with faith. A simple way to look at it is that hope is what we want to happen, and faith is what we do about what we want to happen.

Heb 11:1 *Now faith is the substance of things hoped for, the evidence of things not seen.*

This scripture teaches us that hope is what gives substance to faith. One interesting definition of substance is "the subject matter of thought," which means that in order for me to have faith that something will come to pass, I must first have hopeful thoughts of it coming to pass. As you study the Old Testament scriptures, you will always see that hope comes first. David said in Psalms 119: 81 that as he was waiting for deliverance from God, he was hoping in God's Word. David was still in trouble but he had his hope. David was operating in faith.

Ps 119:81 *My soul fainteth for thy salvation: but I hope in thy word.*

One might say "Well, hope is good, but just because you hope doesn't mean it is going to happen." Let's look at what Paul said about hope:

Rom 5:5 *And hope maketh not ashamed; because the love of God is shed abroad in our hearts by the Holy Ghost which is given unto us.*

This scripture means that God will not disappoint your hope; even if your faith is weak, you must keep on hoping and you won't be ashamed. Whatever we want from God, we must first have hope for it. Hope is simply a desire. In reality, you would not have a desire for something that you did not want in the first place. This principle explains why you cannot allow just anyone to pray for you, because if the person praying for you doesn't have any desire or hope for you to be healed or do better, they will not be able to pray the prayer of faith over your life.

When we have hope and put faith in God's Word, we can expect things to change around us. Look at what Jesus did in Matt 8:16:

Matt 8:16 *When the even was come, they brought unto him many that were possessed with devils: and he cast out the spirits with his word, and healed all that were sick*

1 John 2:14 *. . . I have written unto you, young men, because ye are strong, and the <u>word</u> of God abideth in you, and ye have overcome the wicked one.*

In John 2:14 John uses the word, *"logos,"* saying that "logos "abideth in us. We have available to us the same words that Jesus had. So why doesn't it work for us the way it did for Jesus? If we ever hope to see the Word work for us the way it worked for Jesus, we must realize that when the Word doesn't work, the problem is not with the Word, but with the user of the Word and not using the Word of God in faith.

Heb. 4:12 teaches us that the Word of God is alive, and to be alive means to live for a function, or to function. This is why we should expect things to happen when we use the Word of God. Look how God uses His Word in Ps. 107:20:

Ps. 107:20 *He sent his word, and healed them, and delivered them from their destruction.*

There is truly power in the Word of God, but it will have no effect on us unless we allow that power to work in us and through us. Jesus makes a promise to His disciples concerning His Word in John 8:31-32:

John 8:31-32 *Then said Jesus to those Jews which believed on him, If ye continue in my word, then are ye my disciples indeed;32 And ye shall know the truth, and the truth shall make you free.*

Note that this promise was only made to the people that believed in Jesus. He promised believers that they would be free if they continued in His Word or continued to believe in His Word. We learn from this text that we cannot just believe once we must continue to believe in order to be free. Isn't it funny how we can have Jesus in our lives and still not be free? I am sure you know godly people that are bound by one thing or another. Some people may be bound for a lack of finances, or bound in a bad relationship, or by other bad circumstances. Being bound doesn't mean you are not saved, it just means you are not free. God said it through the prophet Hosea like this:

Hosea 4:6 *My people are destroyed for lack of knowledge: . . . .*

Not having knowledge of God or His Word does not keep us from belonging to God, but it does keep us from being free and enjoying the things of God. This is why we must take time to learn the Word of God and how to obey it. Not only are there advantages to learning how the Word works, there are also disadvantages to not learning how the Word works

Prov 13:13 *Whoso despiseth the word shall be destroyed: but he that feareth the commandment shall be rewarded.*

To despise something means to treat it as worthless and as nothing. We certainly do not want to think that way about the Word of God. We must always remember that the Word works. It can work for us or against us, but it is going to work. Have you ever thought that maybe some of the things going wrong in your life are because you have not doing what the Word say and it is working against you?

The Word Becomes

One of the main reasons God wants us to watch our words is because words have the ability to become things. We certainly don't want things showing up in our life, and then wonder where they came from. Once again we see that this ability that the Word has can work for us or against us. Let's look at how God used the Word to work for Him:

Ps 33:6 *By the word of the Lord were the heavens made; and all the host of them by the breath of his mouth.*

Heb 11:3 *Through faith we understand that the worlds were framed by the word of God, so that things which are seen were not made of things which do appear.*

In everything that God has done, or will do, He uses the Word. When God brought salvation to men, He used the Word to make a body for Jesus. John says in John Chapter 1:

John 1:14 *And the Word was made flesh, and dwelt among us, (and we beheld his glory, the glory as of the only begotten of the Father,) full of grace and truth.*

God's words produced what He said because God had faith in His Word and God believed what He said. Just as God's words produced for Him, our words will produce for us if we believe what we say, and sometimes even when we don't believe what we say.

God's voice in the earth

God wants His people to give Him their voice in the earth. We are God's mouthpiece; we speak for Him. When we speak for God, we can expect God to back us up. Look at what God did for Moses in Exodus. Moses was speaking on behalf of God, so God responded and did what Moses said.

Ex 8:13 And the Lord did according to the word of Moses; and the frogs died out of the houses, out of the villages, and out of the fields.

Ex 8:31 And the Lord did according to the word of Moses; and he removed the swarms of flies from Pharaoh, from his servants, and from his people; there remained not one.

We see this same thing in 1 Kings where Elijah was God's mouthpiece and he spoke for God:

1 Kings 17:1 And Elijah the Tishbite, who was of the inhabitants of Gilead, said unto Ahab, As the Lord God of Israel liveth, before whom I stand, there shall not be dew nor rain these years, but according to my word.

Notice how Elijah said: "*but according to my word.*" Elijah spoke with confidence. He knew that God had his back and that God would do what He said. Throughout the bible we find instances where God had people speak on His behalf. When we speak what God speaks, we do not have to wonder whether or not it will come to pass. We must understand that it is not our responsibility to bring God's Word to pass; that responsibility belongs to God.

Will God's Word come to pass?

Have you ever heard someone say "You never know what God is going to do"? When I hear people say that, I know that they haven't read their bible. If you want to know what God is going to do, just take up the bible and read it. God is going to do just what He said He is going to do. We may not know when God is going to do it. Or even how He is going to do it, but we can know that He is going to do. Sometimes we may find it hard to believe some of the things that God said He is going to do, but we must remember we are talking about God, not man.

Moses himself found it hard to believe God when God said He was going to feed the children of Israel meat for one month, and God had to remind him who He was:

Num 11:23 *And the Lord said unto Moses, Is the Lord's hand waxed short? thou shalt see now whether my word shall come to pass unto thee or not.*

Learning to rightly divide the Word of God is the key to how to work the Word in your life. It is important to remember that some of the things in the Word of God are conditional, meaning that if you do this, then God will do that. There are other things in the Word of God that God has already promised He is going to do, and we are just beneficiaries of His promise.

Deut 9:5 *Not for thy righteousness, or for the uprightness of thine heart, dost thou go to possess their land: but for the wickedness of these nations the Lord thy God doth drive them out from before thee, and that he may perform the word which the Lord sware unto thy fathers, Abraham, Isaac, and Jacob.*

God is very clear throughout Deut. Chapter 9 that He were going to bring the children of Israel into the Promised Land not because of their righteousness or anything good that they had done, but because He had sworn to Abraham, Isaac, and Jacob that He would give their descendants that land. God were acting to fulfil His Word. God's Word will be fulfilled and it will come to pass. We are all called to fulfil the Word of God in our lives. Paul said that he became a minister to fulfil the Word of God:

Col 1:25 *Whereof I am made a minister, according to the dispensation of God which is given to me for you, to fulfil the word of God;*

God made a promise to David which will last forever, and we all reap the benefits of that promise:

2 Sam 7:16 *And thine house and thy kingdom shall be established for ever before thee: thy throne shall be established for ever.*

God's Word is tried

The Word of God is great, true, and forever. The bible is full of great things and promises to the people of God. But I want to caution you not to think that just because God said you have a right to something that you are going to have it. God's Word must be tried in our life, it must be tested. We must trust that what God said will come to pass, but only as we act on what God has said. We must have the same mindset that David had when it comes to the Word of God, which is that the Word of God is perfect and right. That means that if the Word is not working in our lives, there is nothing wrong with the Word, so the problem must be with us.

Ps 18:30 *As for God, his way is perfect: the word of the Lord is tried: he is a buckler to all those that trust in him.*

David lets us know that when the Word of God is tried in our life, we must continue to trust in the Word. We also see another example of this in Ps. 105:19:

Ps 105:19 *Until the time that his word came: the word of the Lord tried him.*

This scripture is speaking about Joseph. God had given Joseph some dreams and had showed him that he would be great in the land. But God did not tell Joseph about the problems he would have before this happened. *Until the time that his word came*: Joseph was beaten by his brothers, thrown in a pit, sold into slavery, assumed by his father to be dead for many years, falsely accused of rape, and thrown in jail. Even with everything that happened to Joseph, he continued to hold on to the dream that God gave him. Even when Joseph was tried, he kept believing what God had shown him.

God's Word is truth

How many things in this life can you really count on? You won't find many, but you can always count on the truth of God's Word. God's Word is true and His work is done in truth. God has not done anything in the dark or in a closet.

Ps 33:4 *For the word of the Lord is right; and all his works are done in truth.*

Pr 30:5 Every word of God is pure: he is a shield unto them that put their trust in him.

This is why God is so predictable because He tells you everything He is going to do. If we have the patience to continue to stand on God's Word, we will be victorious in everything we endeavor to do. The bible says it is settled, all we have to do is wait for it to manifest.

Ps 119:89 For ever, O Lord, thy word is settled in heaven.

Chapter II Scriptures

Rom 13:1 Let *every soul be subject unto the higher powers. For there is no power but of God: the powers that be are ordained of God.*

Gen 1:1 *In the beginning God created the Heaven and the earth.*

Rev 12:10 *And I heard a loud voice saying in heaven, Now is come salvation, and strength, and the kingdom of our God, and the power of his Christ: for the accuser of our brethren is cast down, which accused them before our God day and night.*

Matt 8:5-10 *And when Jesus was entered into Capernaum, there came unto him a centurion, beseeching him,6 And saying, Lord, my servant lieth at home sick of the palsy, grievously tormented.7 And Jesus saith unto him, I will come and heal him.8 The centurion answered and said, Lord, I am not worthy that thou shouldest come under my roof: but speak the word only, and my servant shall be healed.9 For I am a man under authority, having soldiers under me: and I say to this man, Go, and he goeth; and to another, Come, and he cometh; and to my servant, Do this, and he doeth it.10 When Jesus heard it, he marvelled, and said to them that followed, Verily I say unto you, I have not found so great faith, no, not in Israel.*

Luke 4:35-36 *And Jesus rebuked him, saying, Hold thy peace, and come out of him. And when the devil had thrown him in the midst, he came out of him, and hurt him not.36 And they were all amazed, and spake among themselves, saying, What a word is this! for with authority and power he commandeth the unclean spirits, and they come out*

Mark 11:22 And Jesus answering saith unto them, Have faith in God.*

Eccl 8:4 *Where the word of a king is, there is power: and who may say unto him, What doest thou?*

Rom 10:17 *So then faith cometh by hearing, and hearing by the word of God.*

John 1:1 In the beginning was the Word, and the Word was with God, and the Word was God.*

Rom 12:3-4 *For I say, through the grace given unto me, to every man that is among you, not to think of himself more highly than he ought to think; but to think soberly, according as God hath dealt to every man the measure of faith.*

Heb 11:1 *Now faith is the substance of things hoped for, the evidence of things not seen.*

Ps 119:81 *My soul fainteth for thy salvation: but I hope in thy word.*

Rom 5:5 *And hope maketh not ashamed; because the love of God is shed abroad in our hearts by the Holy Ghost which is given unto us.*

Matt 8:16 *When the even was come, they brought unto him many that were possessed with devils: and he cast out the spirits with his word, and healed all that were sick:*

1 John 2:14*I have written unto you, fathers, because ye have known him that is from the beginning. I have written unto you, young men, because ye are strong, and the word of God abideth in you, and ye have overcome the wicked one*

Ps 107:20*He sent his word, and healed them, and delivered them from their destructions.*

John 8:31-32 *Then said Jesus to those Jews which believed on him, If ye continue in my word, then are ye my disciples indeed;32 And ye shall know the truth, and the truth shall make you free.*

Hos 4:6 *My people are destroyed for lack of knowledge: because thou hast rejected knowledge, I will also reject thee, that thou shalt be no priest to me: seeing thou hast forgotten the law of thy God, I will also forget thy children.*

Prov 13:13 *Whoso despiseth the word shall be destroyed: but he that feareth the commandment shall be rewarded.*

Ps 33:6 *By the word of the Lord were the heavens made; and all the host of them by the breath of his mouth.*

Heb 11:3 *Through faith we understand that the worlds were framed by the word of God, so that things which are seen were not made of things which do appear.*

John 1:14 *And the Word was made flesh, and dwelt among us, (and we beheld his glory, the glory as of the only begotten of the Father,) full of grace and truth.*

Ex 8:13 *And the Lord did according to the word of Moses; and the frogs died out of the houses, out of the villages, and out of the fields.*

Ex 8:31 *And the Lord did according to the word of Moses; and he removed the swarms of flies from Pharaoh, from his servants, and from his people; there remained not one.*

1 Kings 17:1 *And Elijah the Tishbite, who was of the inhabitants of Gilead, said unto Ahab, As the Lord God of Israel liveth, before whom I stand, there shall not be dew nor rain these years, but according to my word.*

Num 11:23 *And the Lord said unto Moses, Is the Lord's hand waxed short? thou shalt see now whether my word shall come to pass unto thee or not.*

Deut 9:5 *Not for thy righteousness, or for the uprightness of thine heart, dost thou go to possess their land: but for the wickedness of these nations the Lord thy God doth drive them out from before thee, and that he may perform the word which the Lord sware unto thy fathers, Abraham, Isaac, and Jacob.*

Col 1:25 *Whereof I am made a minister, according to the dispensation of God which is given to me for you, to fulfil the word of God;*

2 Sam 7:16 *And thine house and thy kingdom shall be established for ever before thee: thy throne shall be established for ever*

Ps 18:30 *As for God, his way is perfect: the word of the Lord is tried: he is a buckler to all those that trust in him.*

Ps 105:19 *Until the time that his word came: the word of the Lord tried him.*

Ps 33: 4 *For the word of the Lord is right; and all his works are done in truth.*

Pr 30: 5 *Every word of God is pure: he is a shield unto them that put their trust in him*

Chapter III

Listen; God is Speaking

God speaks

God is always speaking, but it is up to us to listen. What is God saying when He speaks? God speaks to us about everything, but if we are not familiar with God, we will not recognize His voice. Have you ever noticed that a certain person can call your name and, even if you are in a crowded room and can't see them, you will know who called you because you are familiar with their voice? That is the way we should familiarize ourselves with the voice of God. Jesus tells us in John 10: 27:

John 10:27 My sheep hear my voice, and I know them, and they follow me:

One of the reasons God speaks to us is to give us directions. Direction from God is vital, because God knows everything. I read a bumper sticker once that said "Don't worry about tomorrow, because God is already there." If you are going to take direction from someone, who better to take it from than someone who knows everything and has already been where you are going? The primary way that God will speak to us is through His Word.

In Ps. 119, which is what I like to call the Word Psalm, David speaks very highly of God's Word. As children of God we must realize that the most important thing to us is the Word of God. David said in Ps. 119:100 that because of the direction that he received from the Word, he knew more than his teachers. David recognized that he received directions from the Word. David also knew that the Word kept him from evil. In Ps. 119:103 David even called the Word sweet, which means he loved to obey it. Most of the Christians I know look at obeying the Word of God as a great sacrifice.

Ps 119:105 *Thy word is a lamp unto my feet, and a light unto my path.*

The Word of God is a lamp that lights up our feet so we will know where to step next. When you walk by the Word of God, it requires faith. When we follow God's Word, we must believe God every step of the way. We may not be able to see what tomorrow holds, but whatever it is, we know God will be there.

I have always been fascinated by David. David was a man of war, a warrior, a mighty man, and at the same time he was a psalmist who wrote poetry. David was a man of passion and whatever he did he did it with passion. When David was watching his father's sheep, he did it with passion. When he fought, he fought with passion. Whether David was writing poetry or playing musical instruments, he had passion about it. I believe the one thing that made David so great was his total reliance on God.

Ps 119:133 *Order my steps in thy word: and let not any iniquity have dominion over me.*

Notice how David seeks Gods directions. David knew what the Word of God said, but he did not want to misunderstand it, so he asked God to order his steps in the Word. David did not ask God to order his steps to victory over his enemies. No, David wasn't worried about his enemies.

David did not want to displease God. This is why, I believe, God called David a man after His own heart.

As we seek directions from God, we must be ready and willing to obey them when He gives them to us. Have you ever been driving somewhere and you got lost and asked someone for directions, but you didn't believe what they told you, so you didn't follow the directions? Most of the time when God gives us directions, His directions don't make any sense to us in the natural, but we must remember God is not natural, He is supernatural. Let's look at an example of God's directions in the bible:

1 Kings 18:1 *And it came to pass after many days, that the word of the Lord came to Elijah in the third year, saying, Go, shew thyself unto Ahab; and I will send rain upon the earth.*

In this text Elijah was hiding from Ahab the king. Ahab had been looking for Elijah for many days because Ahab felt that Elijah was an enemy of Israel, and he wanted to kill him. God then gives Elijah instructions to go show himself to Ahab. I can image that Elijah must have thought, "God, are you sure?" When we learn to trust God, we find out that how things turn out when we follow God's instructions is not as important as whether or not we obey God's instructions. Samuel told Saul that to obey is better than sacrifice.

1 Sam 15:22 . . . . *Behold, to obey is better than sacrifice, and to hearken than the fat of rams.*

Why is obeying better that sacrifice? Simply put, if I obey, I will not have to make a sacrifice.

God speaks through man

Why does God speak through man? God speaks through man because man has dominion in the earth. God has always used man to do His will in the earth. Because God is wiser than man, He knows what man needs now, and what man will need in the future. God has already looked ahead and seen what we will need. God must use man to speak into man's future in the earth.

As David lay on his death bed, God continued to use him to speak into the earth. God used David to teach us how a ruler must conduct himself, ruling in the fear of the lord. God also lets the ruler know what the end result will be if he rules in the fear of the lord.

2 Sam 23:2-4 *The Spirit of the Lord spake by me, and his word was in my tongue.3 The God of Israel said, the Rock of Israel spake to me, He that ruleth over men must be just, ruling in the fear of God.4 And he shall be as the light of the morning, when the sun riseth, even a morning without clouds; as the tender grass springing out of the earth by clear shining after rain.*

Because God used David to speak these words, a ruler can now have faith that God's words will come to pass in their life if they rule in the fear of the lord. Throughout the Old Testament, God has used many people to speak to the kings of the earth. God used Shemaiah, in I Kings 12, to speak to King Rehoboam because God wanted to prevent something from taking place:

1 Kings 12:22-24 But the word of God came unto Shemaiah the man of God, saying, 23 Speak unto Rehoboam, the son of Solomon, king of Judah, and unto all the house of Judah and Benjamin, and to the remnant of the people, saying, 24 Thus saith the Lord, Ye shall not go up, nor fight against your brethren the children of Israel: return every man to his house; for this thing is from me. They hearkened therefore to the word of the Lord, and returned to depart, according to the word of the Lord.

Let's look at another example of how God gets His Word into the earth. In I Kings 13: 1-5, the bible doesn't even give us the name of the man God used, it simply says "a man of God". We can understand from this that the person is not what's important; it is the words that must be spoken by man that are important.

1 Kings 13:1-5 And, behold, there came a man of God out of Judah by the word of the Lord unto Bethel: and Jeroboam stood by the altar to burn incense. 2 And he cried against the altar in the word of the Lord, and said, O altar, altar, thus saith the Lord; Behold, a child shall be born unto the house of David, Josiah by name; and upon thee shall he offer the priests of the high places that burn incense upon thee, and men's bones shall be burnt upon thee. 3 And he gave a sign the same day, saying, This is the sign which the Lord hath spoken; Behold, the altar shall be rent, and the

ashes that are upon it shall be poured out.4 And it came to pass, when king
Jeroboam heard the saying of the man of God, which had cried against
the altar in Bethel, that he put forth his hand from the altar, saying, Lay
hold on him. And his hand, which he put forth against him, dried up, so
that he could not pull it in again to him.5 The altar also was rent, and
the ashes poured out from the altar, according to the sign which the man
of God had given by the word of the Lord.

As we continue to read about this man of God, we learn that he was
given some unusual instructions by God: he should not eat or drink, and
he was not to go to anyone's home.

1 Kings 13:7-9 And the king said unto the man of God, Come home with
me, and refresh thyself, and I will give thee a reward.8 And the man of
God said unto the king, If thou wilt give me half thine house, I will not go
in with thee, neither will I eat bread nor drink water in this place:9 For
so was it charged me by the word of the Lord, saying, Eat no bread, nor
drink water, nor turn again by the same way that thou camest.

When the king offered the man of God to come home with him, the
man of God knew better. But as we continue to read, we see that this man
was fooled by a fellow prophet.

1 Kings 13:16-25 And he said, I may not return with thee, nor go in with
thee: neither will I eat bread nor drink water with thee in this place:17
For it was said to me by the word of the Lord, Thou shalt eat no bread nor
drink water there, nor turn again to go by the way that thou camest.18 He

said unto him, I am a prophet also as thou art; and an angel spake unto me by the word of the Lord, saying, Bring him back with thee into thine house, that he may eat bread and drink water. But he lied unto him.19 So he went back with him, and did eat bread in his house, and drank water.20 And it came to pass, as they sat at the table, that the word of the Lord came unto the prophet that brought him back:21 And he cried unto the man of God that came from Judah, saying, Thus saith the Lord, Forasmuch as thou hast disobeyed the mouth of the Lord, and hast not kept the commandment which the Lord thy God commanded thee,22 But camest back, and hast eaten bread and drunk water in the place, of the which the Lord did say to thee, Eat no bread, and drink no water; thy carcase shall not come unto the sepulchre of thy fathers.23 And it came to pass, after he had eaten bread, and after he had drunk, that he saddled for him the ass, to wit, for the prophet whom he had brought back.24 And when he was gone, a lion met him by the way, and slew him: and his carcase was cast in the way, and the ass stood by it, the lion also stood by the carcase.

The lesson we learn from this man is that we must listen when God speaks. There will always be things that come up in our lives that will try to pull us away from doing what the Word of God says, but don't fall for it, because it will take you down the wrong path.

There are times in our lives when God's will is not clear to us, and we must seek God's will. Learning to seek God's Word, especially in times of decision, is a sign of wisdom. Jehoshaphat, king of Judah, made a habit of seeking the Word of the Lord when decisions had to be made. In 2 Kings Chapter 3, Jehoshaphat had to make a decision about whether or not to go with Ahab, so he seeks the Word of the Lord. Jehoshaphat was looking for a prophet that carried the Word of the Lord.

> *2 Kings 3:11-12 But Jehoshaphat said, Is there not here a prophet of the Lord, that we may inquire of the Lord by him? And one of the king of Israel's servants answered and said, Here is Elisha the son of Shaphat, which poured water on the hands of Elijah.12 And Jehoshaphat said, The word of the Lord is with him. So the king of Israel and Jehoshaphat and the king of Edom went down to him.*

We must learn to receive the Word of the Lord as the Word from God. We cannot be fooled by what men say. I thank God that, because of Jesus, we are New Covenant Christians and we can go before God on our own and seek His will.

God's Word lives

God's Word is not just something we read to make us feel good about ourselves. God's Word is alive and well. There are certain characteristics that living things have. If something is living it will continue growing, it will have personality and purpose. The Word of God has a personality and manners and it must be invited in. God will never force Himself on us against our will. God's Word has a way that it will work and a way it will not work. In order for God's Word to work in our lives, we must obey it and do what it says. Col. 3:16 said we must let the Word dwell in us. Note the word "let," which means "allow". God has a desire to live richly in us with all wisdom. God's Word is a teacher; it teaches us and makes us happy. Something that is dead cannot do that.

Col 3:16 *Let the word of Christ dwell in you richly in all wisdom; teaching and admonishing one another in psalms and hymns and spiritual songs, singing with grace in your hearts to*

Heb 4:12 said the Word is quick, which means alive. The Word of God can read our minds; it can discern what is in our spirit from what is in our soul. The Word of God not only discerns the thoughts of the heart, but it also discern the intents of the heart. Wow, isn't that awesome?

Heb 4:12 *For the word of God is quick, and powerful, and sharper than any twoedged sword, piercing even to the dividing asunder of soul and spirit, and of the joints and marrow, and is a discerner of the thoughts and intents of the heart.*

With all of these functions that the Word of God accomplishes, there is no doubt in my mind that the Word of God is alive. God's Word is a living word and God meant for His Word to be alive in us and to work for us. God Himself uses His Word. God used His Word to create the earth. God also uses the Word to run errands for Him:

Ps 147:15 *He sendeth forth his commandment upon earth: his word runneth very swiftly.*

God's Word makes merry

Have you ever been feeling down, having a bad day, and someone said something to you and it made you feel good? Words have the power to affect our mood. We can read God's Word every day to make ourselves feel merry. We can also speak God's Word to someone else to make them feel merry. Just think of it like this: when you leave home in the morning, you carry the power to determine whether someone has a good day or a bad day.

Prov 12:25 *Heaviness in the heart of man maketh it stoop: but a good word maketh it glad.*

We truly do have life and death in the power of our tongue. I understand now why my mother always said "if you can't say something good about someone, don't say anything at all.

CHAPTER III SCRIPTURES

John 10:27 My sheep hear my voice, and I know them, and they follow me:

Ps 119:105 Thy word is a lamp unto my feet, and a light unto my path.

Ps 119:133 Order my steps in thy word: and let not any iniquity have dominion over me.

1 Kings 18:1 And it came to pass after many days, that the word of the Lord came to Elijah in the third year, saying, Go, shew thyself unto Ahab; and I will send rain upon the earth.

1 Sam 15:22 And Samuel said, Hath the Lord as great delight in burnt offerings and sacrifices, as in obeying the voice of the Lord? Behold, to obey is better than sacrifice, and to hearken than the fat of rams.

2 Sam 23:2-4 The Spirit of the Lord spake by me, and his word was in my tongue. 3 The God of Israel said, the Rock of Israel spake to me, He that ruleth over men must be just, ruling in the fear of God. 4 And he shall be as the light of the morning, when the sun riseth, even a morning without clouds; as the tender grass springing out of the earth by clear shining after rain.

1 Kings 12:22-24 But the word of God came unto Shemaiah the man of God, saying, 23 Speak unto Rehoboam, the son of Solomon, king of Judah, and unto all the house of Judah and Benjamin, and to the remnant of the people, saying, 24 Thus saith the Lord, Ye shall not go up, nor fight against your brethren the children of Israel: return every man to his house; for this thing is from me. They hearkened therefore to the word of the Lord, and returned to depart, according to the word of the Lord.

1 Kings 13:1-5 And, behold, there came a man of God out of Judah by the word of the Lord unto Bethel: and Jeroboam stood by the altar to burn incense. 2 And he cried against the altar in the word of the Lord, and said, O altar, altar, thus saith the Lord; Behold, a child shall be born unto the house of David, Josiah by name; and upon thee shall he offer the priests of the high places that burn incense upon thee, and men's bones shall be burnt upon thee. 3 And he gave a sign the same day, saying, This is the sign which the Lord hath spoken; Behold, the altar shall be rent, and the ashes that are upon it shall be poured out.

4 And it came to pass, when king Jeroboam heard the saying of the man of God, which had cried against the altar in Bethel, that he put forth his hand from the altar, saying, Lay hold on him. And his hand, which he put forth against him, dried up,

so that he could not pull it in again to him.5 The altar also was rent, and the ashes poured out from the altar, according to the sign which the man of God had given by the word of the Lord.

1 Kings 13:7-9*And the king said unto the man of God, Come home with me, and refresh thyself, and I will give thee a reward.8 And the man of God said unto the king, If thou wilt give me half thine house, I will not go in with thee, neither will I eat bread nor drink water in this place:9 For so was it charged me by the word of the Lord, saying, Eat no bread, nor drink water, nor turn again by the same way that thou camest.*

1 Kings 13:16-25*And he said, I may not return with thee, nor go in with thee: neither will I eat bread nor drink water with thee in this place:17 For it was said to me by the word of the Lord, Thou shalt eat no bread nor drink water there, nor turn again to go by the way that thou camest.18 He said unto him, I am a prophet also as thou art; and an angel spake unto me by the word of the Lord, saying, Bring him back with thee into thine house, that he may eat bread and drink water. But he lied unto him.19 So he went back with him, and did eat bread in his house, and drank water.20 And it came to pass, as they sat at the table, that the word of the Lord came unto the prophet that brought him back:21 And he cried unto the man of God that came from Judah, saying, Thus saith the Lord, Forasmuch as thou hast disobeyed the mouth of the Lord, and hast not kept the commandment which the Lord thy God commanded thee,22 But camest back, and hast eaten bread and drunk water in the place, of the which the Lord did say to thee, Eat no bread, and drink no water; thy carcase shall not come unto the sepulchre of thy fathers.23 And it came to pass, after he had eaten bread, and after he had drunk, that he saddled for him the ass, to wit, for the prophet whom he had brought back.24 And when he was gone, a lion met him by the way, and slew him: and his carcase was cast in the way, and the ass stood by it, the lion also stood by the carcase.*

2 Kings 3:11-12 *But Jehoshaphat said, Is there not here a prophet of the Lord, that we may inquire of the Lord by him? And one of the king of Israel's servants answered and said, Here is Elisha the son of Shaphat, which poured water on the hands of Elijah.12 And Jehoshaphat said, The word of the Lord is with him. So the king of Israel and Jehoshaphat and the king of Edom went down to him.*

Col 3:16 *Let the word of Christ dwell in you richly in all wisdom; teaching and admonishing one another in psalms and hymns and spiritual songs, singing with grace in your hearts to*

Heb 4:12 *For the word of God is quick, and powerful, and sharper than any twoedged sword, piercing even to the dividing asunder of soul and spirit, and of the joints and marrow, and is a discerner of the thoughts and intents of the heart.*

Ps 147:15 *He sendeth forth his commandment upon earth: his word runneth very swiftly.*

Prov 12:25 *Heaviness in the heart of man maketh it stoop: but a good word maketh it glad*

CHAPTER IV

UNDERSTANDING THE WORD

Say it again: I didn't understand

Prov 4:7 *Wisdom is the principal thing; therefore get wisdom: and with all thy getting get understanding.*

Understanding is critical in anything that we do, because it doesn't matter how much we know if we don't understand how to use what we know. What we take away from the Word of God will be determined by the degree of our understanding.

Matt 13:23 *But he that received seed into the good ground is he that heareth the word, and understandeth it; which also beareth fruit, and bringeth forth, some an hundredfold, some sixty, some thirty.*

Notice the above text said "*some an hundredfold, some sixty, some thirty.*" After reading this you must ask yourself the question, what determines whether we get hundredfold, sixty, or thirty? The answer is our degree of understanding.

The main way we can increase our understanding is to study, study, and study. Studying the Word of God is what the bible tells us to do.

2 Tim 2:15 *Study to shew thyself approved unto God, a workman that needeth not to be ashamed, rightly dividing the word of truth.*

We must show ourselves approved unto God, and the way we do that is by studying the Word of God. The Word of God must be rightly divided, and the way we learn to rightly divide the Word is by studying. I have always found it interesting that we understand that an employer can expect us to meet certain requirements for a job position, but when it comes to the things of God, we feel we do not have to meet any requirements.

What makes understanding so great is that understanding is constantly giving birth to more understanding.

Prov 16:22 *Understanding is a wellspring of life unto him that hath it: . . . .*

Prov. 16:22 uses the term *"wellspring,"* which means it is constantly moving and bringing in more understanding. When we begin to understand the things of God, it will produce joy in our lives. We cannot truly have joy without understanding. The bible teaches us that grace and peace come through knowledge.

2 Peter 1:2 *Grace and peace be multiplied unto you through the knowledge of God, and of Jesus our Lord,*

Sure, we can shout and be happy, but sooner or later we are going to want to know what we are shouting about. That's when understanding and knowledge come in to play.

Why are you so happy?

Why does understanding make us so happy? When we understand what is happening, we feel that everything is going to be alright, and we know that we will come out on top. Nehemiah Chapter 8 gives us a great example of how understanding makes us happy. Verse 1 says that the people gathered themselves together as one to hear the Word of God. Verse 2 says that both men and women, and all that could hear with understanding, came together. Please note that when they came together, they had a desire to understand the Word. One of the first things we learn about understanding is that it must be desired. Nehemiah Chapter 8 goes on to say that they read the law of God distinctly, and gave the sense, which caused them to understand the reading. This means that they took some time to teach what they read. We also learn from this text that the people wept when they heard the words of the law. Understanding will always bring an emotional response. Looking at verse 10, we see another result from understanding: "joy":

Neh.8:10 *Then he said unto them, Go your way, eat the fat, and drink the sweet, and send portions unto them for whom nothing is prepared: for this day is holy unto our Lord: neither be ye sorry; for the joy of the Lord is your strength.*

Understanding will cause us to change the way we think, the way we see things, and what we do. A careful study of Neh. Chapters 8-13 revels the changes that Israel made because of the understanding that they got, and I believe understanding will do the same for us.

Do I really understand?

Ps 119:73 Thy hands have made me and fashioned me: give me understanding, that I may learn thy commandments.

The more I study about David, the more I realize that the most important thing to David was to please God. David knew the only way to please God was to keep His commandments. David also realized that because of his nature, keeping God's commandments was not just naturally going to happen. David asked God to give him understanding about how he was fashioned. David was seeking to understand why he did the things he did, and why he felt the way he felt. David felt that if he could understand himself, he would be in a better position to learn God's commandments. Wow, what an awesome way to think.

Ps 119:33-35 Teach me, O Lord, the way of thy statutes; and I shall keep it unto the end.34 Give me understanding, and I shall keep thy law; yea, I shall observe it with my whole heart.35 Make me to go in the path of thy commandments; for therein do I delight.

Again we see that David's focus and obsession is on pleasing God. David is teaching us something that most of us don't learn easily, and that is that only God can show us what pleases Him. Can you imagine how much better we could get along with others if we asked them, and they told us what they like? When we have problems with each other, it is usually because of a misunderstanding, where something we thought about someone wasn't correct. David is telling us to ask God and God will tell us how to please Him!

Ps 119:27 Make me to understand the way of thy precepts: so shall I talk of thy wondrous works.

Understanding what you have

There is an old saying that says, "You don't miss the water until the well runs dry." That is just another way of saying that if we don't understand what we have then we will not appreciate it. This saying is so true, and it is also a principle of the kingdom of God.

Matt 13:19 When any one heareth the word of the kingdom, and understandeth it not, then cometh the wicked one, and catcheth away that which was sown in his heart. This is he which received seed by the way side.

One of the main reasons that the Word does not work for us is because we do not give it time to take root and grow in our hearts. When we hear the Word and we do not understand what we have heard, then the enemy comes and steals it away from us. The enemy doesn't have much of a problem stealing the Word from us if we don't understand what we have.

If something is of no value to me, and someone tries to rob me and take it from me, I am not going to put up much of a fight. We must understand that the Word of God is priceless and eternal. The bible calls the Word of God incorruptible seed, and seed must be planted, watered, and nurtured, before it grows.

1 Peter 1:23 Being born again, not of corruptible seed, but of incorruptible, by the word of God, which liveth and abideth for ever.

The enemy does not want you to retain the Word of God in your heart, because he knows that it will grow and then you will be harder to deal with; he won't be able to get you to believe just anything. Every attack of the enemy is because he is after the Word that you heard and believed. You may have a lack of money and feel the enemy is holding your money, but know that the devil doesn't need money. Or you may have car problems, but he doesn't need a car either. The devil's whole job is to steal the Word of God from you before it grows in your heart and produce fruit in your life.

Don't be deceived

Have you ever heard the saying, "The same thing that makes you laugh will make you cry"? If we don't understand the Word and what it means, we can easily be deceived by the very same Word that shows us the way. God commands us to study the Word. The command to study the Word of God is not just for the preacher, but for every believer. Proverbs 14:15 said:

Prov 14:15 *The simple believeth every word: but the prudent man looketh well to his going.*

This text teaches us that what we do is just as important as our believing. Only "the simple" believe but don't do anything about what they believe. This is a principle we see throughout the bible. In the book of James we see the same thing:

James 2:20 *But wilt thou know, O vain man, that faith without works is dead?*

I believe that we as the Body of Christ have been somewhat deceived in thinking that all we have to do is just believe, but what we believe will be shown by what we do about it. Believing is great, but the bible teaches us that God will bless the work of our hands; that means we must do something.

Being deceived about the Word of God is not just a possibility, it is very likely to happen. In Eph. 5:6 God warns us about this:

Eph 5:6 *Let no man deceive you with vain words: for because of these things cometh the wrath of God upon the children of disobedience.*

One of the biggest falsehoods that have been taught is that when we give our life to Christ, all of our troubles will go away. In Col.2:1-4, Paul taught that we could receive comfort in our troubles, not because the troubles would go away, but because we would be knitted together in love and understanding. The thing that gives us joy in trouble is that we know that God has all treasures of wisdom and knowledge.

Col 2:1-4 *For I would that ye knew what great conflict I have for you, and for them at Laodicea, and for as many as have not seen my face in the flesh;2 That their hearts might be comforted, being knit together in love, and unto all riches of the full assurance of understanding, to the acknowledgement of the mystery of God, and of the Father, and of Christ;3 In whom are hid all the treasures of wisdom and knowledge.4 And this I say, lest any man should beguile you with enticing words.*

The Word's Judges

In spite of the real possibility that others may use the Word of God to deceive us, we as Christians are still held accountable by God for how we respond to the Word of God. I often find myself saying to people, "The Word of God is true and it can work for you or against you." I believe that is exactly what Jesus meant when He spoke in Luke 12:47-48:

Luke 12:47-48 *And that servant, which knew his lord's will, and prepared not himself, neither did according to his will, shall be beaten with many stripes.48 But he that knew not, and did commit things worthy of stripes, shall be beaten with few stripes. For unto whomsoever much is given, of him shall be much required: and to whom men have committed much, of him they will ask the more.*

If you know something, then you are responsible for what you know. This is also a principle of the Kingdom of God. This principle works great if you are having problems forgiving someone who has wronged you. When I realize that someone that has wronged me didn't really know what they were doing, then I can't hold them accountable for their action. That is the principle Jesus used to forgive those that crucified Him.

Luke 23:34 *Then said Jesus, Father, forgive them; for they know not what they do. And they parted his raiment, and cast lots.*

When one comes to this realization, one might say, "You mean I could get in bigger trouble with God by listening to the Word of God and not obeying, than by not listening to the Word of God?" In a sense that could be true, especially when you realize that you will be judged on what you know. Jesus talks more about this John 12:47-50:

John 12:47-50 *And if any man hear my words, and believe not, I judge him not: for I came not to judge the world, but to save the world. 48 He that rejecteth me, and receiveth not my words, hath one that judgeth him: the word that I have spoken, the same shall judge him in the last day. 49 For I have not spoken of myself; but the Father which sent me, he gave me a commandment, what I should say, and what I should speak. 50 And I know that his commandment is life everlasting: whatsoever I speak therefore, even as the Father said unto me, so I speak.*

Jesus told them that He would not judge them, but He said that the words that He spoke would judge them. Jesus goes on to say that the words that He speaks were of the Father and that the Father would judge them. This truth shows us another principle of the kingdom: that which is spoken in the kingdom will reflect the authority that we have. Understanding kingdom principle is vital to functioning in the kingdom, and the reason we want to function in the kingdom of God is because everything that we need is in the kingdom of God.

Matt 12:37 *For by thy words thou shalt be justified, and by thy words thou shalt be condemned.*

CHAPTER IV SCRIPTURES

Prov 4:7 *Wisdom is the principal thing; therefore get wisdom: and with all thy getting get understanding.*

Matt 13:23 *But he that received seed into the good ground is he that heareth the word, and understandeth it; which also beareth fruit, and bringeth forth, some an hundredfold, some sixty, some thirty.*

2 Tim 2:15 *Study to shew thyself approved unto God, a workman that needeth not to be ashamed, rightly dividing the word of truth.*

Prov 16:22*Understanding is a wellspring of life unto him that hath it: but the instruction of fools is folly.*

2 Peter 1:2 *Grace and peace be multiplied unto you through the knowledge of God, and of Jesus our Lord,*

Neh.8:10*Then he said unto them, Go your way, eat the fat, and drink the sweet, and send portions unto them for whom nothing is prepared: for this day is holy unto our Lord: neither be ye sorry; for the joy of the Lord is your strength.*

Ps 119:73 *Thy hands have made me and fashioned me: give me understanding, that I may learn thy commandments.*

Ps 119:33-35 *Teach me, O Lord, the way of thy statutes; and I shall keep it unto the end.34 Give me understanding, and I shall keep thy law; yea, I shall observe it with my whole heart.35 Make me to go in the path of thy commandments; for therein do I delight.*

Ps 119:27*Make me to understand the way of thy precepts: so shall I talk of thy wondrous works.*

Matt 13:19 *When any one heareth the word of the kingdom, and understandeth it not, then cometh the wicked one, and catcheth away that which was sown in his heart. This is he which received seed by the way side.*

1 Peter 1:23*Being born again, not of corruptible seed, but of incorruptible, by the word of God, which liveth and abideth for ever.*

Prov 14:15 *The simple believeth every word: but the prudent man looketh well to his going.*

James 2:20 *But wilt thou know, O vain man, that faith without works is dead?*

Eph 5:6 *Let no man deceive you with vain words: for because of these things cometh the wrath of God upon the children of disobedience.*

Col 2:1-4 *For I would that ye knew what great conflict I have for you, and for them at Laodicea, and for as many as have not seen my face in the flesh;2 That their hearts might be comforted, being knit together in love, and unto all riches of the full assurance of understanding, to the acknowledgement of the mystery of God, and of the Father, and of Christ;3 In whom are hid all the treasures of wisdom and knowledge.4 And this I say, lest any man should beguile you with enticing words.*

Luke 12:47-48 *And that servant, which knew his lord's will, and prepared not himself, neither did according to his will, shall be beaten with many stripes.48 But he that knew not, and did commit things worthy of stripes, shall be beaten with few stripes. For unto whomsoever much is given, of him shall be much required: and to whom men have committed much, of him they will ask the more.*

Luke 23:34 *Then said Jesus, Father, forgive them; for they know not what they do. And they parted his raiment, and cast lots.*

John 12:47-50 *And if any man hear my words, and believe not, I judge him not: for I came not to judge the world, but to save the world. 48 He that rejecteth me, and receiveth not my words, hath one that judgeth him: the word that I have spoken, the same shall judge him in the last day. 49 For I have not spoken of myself; but the Father which sent me, he gave me a commandment, what I should say, and what I should speak.50 And I know that his commandment is life everlasting: whatsoever I speak therefore, even as the Father said unto me, so I speak.*

Matt 12:37 *For by thy words thou shalt be justified, and by thy words thou shalt be condemned.*

Chapter V

According to the Word of the Lord

Learning to speak according to the Word is a process, and it may take some time, depending on how much time you spend in the Word. In James 3:1-2, James teaches us that if we can master our words, we will be perfect men. James said this because he understood that our words always come back to us for good or bad. James lets us know right off that we are not going to master everything, but if we work on our words, we will do well.

James 3:1-2 My brethren, be not many masters, knowing that we shall receive the greater condemnation.2 For in many things we offend all. If any man offend not in word, the same is a perfect man, and able also to bridle the whole body.

Living our life according to the Word not only shows God that we love Him, it also keeps us out of trouble. Most of the time when we study the Word of God, we are seeking what we should do or the way we should go, but often the Word teaches us what not to do or the path not to take. If you have children you have probably said to yourself at least once, "I wish my children would listen to me so they won't make the same mistakes I did."

I believe this is the reason God shows us different people with different personalities in the bible, so we will not only know what to do, but also what not to do. I wonder if God is saying "I wish my children would listen to what they see in the bible so they won't make the same mistakes they did".

If you were to think back over your life and think of every unforeseen thing that happened to you, you would find that it was because you did not do something according to the Word. God gives us instruction not for His benefit, but for ours. Look at what happened to Nadab and Abihu when they did not perform their duties according to the Word of the Lord:

Num 3:4 And Nadab and Abihu died before the Lord, when they offered strange fire before the Lord, in the wilderness of Sinai, ...

Moses in Num. 3:16 obeyed and did what God said:

Num 3:16 And Moses numbered them according to the word of the Lord, as he was commanded.

As we get older, we should get wiser, and hopefully realize that it is always better to do things God's way. But wouldn't it be nice if we could just read the bible and look at what happened to some of them and say, "I am not going to do that".

God said it, not I

If we want to be sure that we speak the truth at all times, all we have to do is say what God said. Saying what God said will ensure that what

57

we say will always come to pass. There are several advantages to speaking God's Word, such as:

- You don't have to worry about backing up what you say
- You know you are speaking the truth
- You know what you say will come to pass, whether you see it or not
- The words in themselves have power

Speaking the Word of God may not always get you the desired effect, especially when you are speaking it to others. Some of the people you speak the Word to may not believe. If you are having problems with people believing what you say when you speak the Word of God, then you are in good company. Jesus had the same problem. Jesus taught us in John Chapter 8 that whoever believes a lie and not the truth does so because of who their father is: the devil. Jesus said in John 8:43 that they did not hear or understand Him.

John 8:43 Why do ye not understand my speech? even because ye cannot hear my word.

Jesus said it is a hereditary problem; their father is the devil.

John 8:44 Ye are of your father the devil, and the lusts of your father ye will do. He was a murderer from the beginning, and abode not in the truth, because there is no truth in him. When he speaketh a lie, he speaketh of his own: for he is a liar, and the father of it.

Notice how Jesus implied that we have a tendency to do like our fathers. I have often heard in the church that we were all children of God, but based on this scripture, we are not all children of God: the devil has some children, too.

Caution: God's Word in use

One of the main things that we should use God's words for is comfort. We must have faith in what God said and faith in what God is saying. Faith in the Word of God will bring us comfort. For too long we have been taught that we use our faith to get God to do things for us, but this is simply not true. Heb. 11: 6 tells us that without faith it is impossible to please God, but it does not say that God is moved by faith.

Heb 11:6 *But without faith it is impossible to please him: . . . .*

A careful study of the Word of God will reveal to us that God's Word will come to pass whether we believe it or not. God gave me a revelation when I began to ask Him, "What is the real purpose of my faith?" God showed me that He did not give me faith to move Him, but He gave me faith so that I wouldn't' move until He showed up: then God drew my attention to Ps.27: 13:

Ps 27:13 *I had fainted, unless I had believed to see the goodness of the Lord in the land of the living.*

Note what David is saying. David is not saying that God showed up and kept him from fainting. David is saying that it was his belief that God would show up that kept him from fainting. The real purpose of our faith is to keep us until God shows up in our situation. God created man and He knows how He put man together. God knows that man needs something to believe in, so God is telling man to believe in Him. This is what faith is, a belief in God. Can you imagine what the Christian life would be like if we didn't believe? If we did not have a belief in God, the devil would probably wipe out all Christians in less than a day.

Without a belief in God, whenever the enemy showed us trouble, we would immediately react and panic. People would be lining up to commit suicide. But because we have faith in the Word of God, even though trouble comes, we know that God will work it out; we can take comfort in that.

Paul shows us the same thing in 1 Thess 4:15-18. Paul gives us God's words that we can take comfort in:

> *1 Thess 4:15-18 For this we say unto you by the word of the Lord, that we which are alive and remain unto the coming of the Lord shall not prevent them which are asleep.16 For the Lord himself shall descend from heaven with a shout, with the voice of the archangel, and with the trump of God: and the dead in Christ shall rise first:17 Then we which are alive and remain shall be caught up together with them in the clouds, to meet the Lord in the air: and so shall we ever be with the Lord.18 Wherefore comfort one another with these words.*

Note in verses 15-17 Paul is telling us some things that are going to happen. Also note that what Paul said is going to happen does not depend on our faith. Paul tells us in verse 18 that we can take comfort in verses 15-17. If I choose not to do like Paul said and I don't take comfort, that does not mean that verses 15-17 won't happen.

Prov 24:10 *If thou faint in the day of adversity, thy strength is small.*

The Word of No Effect

One might ask, "How can the Word of God ever be of no effect?" That is a good question and the answer is, when we don't do the Word. As with anything we do in life, if I don't take advantage of something I can't reap the benefit of it. We must remember that we not only obey the Word because it is the Word of God, but the Word also carries an effect with it. That effect can be either negative if the Word is not kept, or positive if the Word is kept. Jesus brings this to our attention in Mark 7. Jesus points out that God used Moses to give them instructions, but because they did and taught others to do contrary to what God said through Moses, the Word of God had no effect in their life.

Mark 7:10-13 *For Moses said, Honour thy father and thy mother; and, Whoso curseth father or mother, let him die the death:11 But ye say, If a man shall say to his father or mother, It is Corban, that is to say, a gift, by whatsoever thou mightest be profited by me; he shall be free.12 And ye suffer him no more to do ought for his father or his mother;13 Making the word of God of none effect through your tradition, which ye have delivered: and many such like things do ye.*

Another thing that makes the Word of God of no effect in our lives is not understanding the Word of God. How well we understand God's Word will determine the effect that the Word has in our lives. Let's look at how Jesus puts this:

Matt 13:23 *But he that received seed into the good ground is he that heareth the word, and understandeth it; which also beareth fruit, and bringeth forth, some an hundredfold, some sixty, some thirty.*

Notice that Jesus makes it clear that our understanding of the Word will determine our return on the Word, either a thirty, sixty or hundredfold return. This is why a constant study of the Word is so important. We must continue to hear the Word and study the Word on a daily basis so that we can get more understanding.

Prov 4:7 *Wisdom is the principal thing; therefore get wisdom: and with all thy getting get understanding.*

Many times in our lives we do not get the result that we think we should from the Word, but we must understand that the fault is not in the Word. The fault is in us and our understanding. Paul teaches us this in Roman 9. He said it's not that the Word had no effect, it is that they were misrepresenting who they were. They were not Israel and, therefore, they were not in line with the Word.

Rom 9:6-9 *Not as though the word of God hath taken none effect. For they are not all Israel, which are of Israel:7 Neither, because they are* *the seed of Abraham, are they all children: but, In Isaac shall thy seed be called.8 That is, They which are the children of the flesh, these are not the children of God: but the children of the promise are counted for the seed.9 For this is the word of promise, At this time will I come, and Sara shall have a son.*

I believe one of the biggest mistakes that Christians make is assuming that the Word will just naturally come to pass in their life. We must learn to work with the Word. This is what Paul was talking about here:

1 Cor 3:9 For we are labourers together with God: ye are God's husbandry, ye are God's building.

Not only must we believe the Word and do the Word, we must line ourselves up with the Word. Last but not least, we must pray that the Word of God will have free course in our lives.

2 Thess 3:1 Finally, brethren, pray for us, that the word of the Lord may have free course, and be glorified, even as it is with you:

We must remember that God has a plan for every life that He has created, but if we do not pursue the plan of God for our life, it will not come to pass. If we just say "whatever will be will be," we will find ourselves taking the path of least resistance, and when we take the path of least resistance, we will never walk fully in what God has for us.

Chapter V Scriptures

James 3:1-2 *My brethren, be not many masters, knowing that we shall receive the greater condemnation. 2 For in many things we offend all. If any man offend not in word, the same is a perfect man, and able also to bridle the whole body.*

Num 3:4 *And Nadab and Abihu died before the Lord, when they offered strange fire before the Lord, in the wilderness of Sinai, and they had no children: and Eleazar and Ithamar ministered in the priest's office in the sight of Aaron their father.*

Num 3:16 *And Moses numbered them according to the word of the Lord, as he was commanded*

John 8:43 *Why do ye not understand my speech? even because ye cannot hear my word.*

John 8:44 *Ye are of your father the devil, and the lusts of your father ye will do. He was a murderer from the beginning, and abode not in the truth, because there is no truth in him. When he speaketh a lie, he speaketh of his own: for he is a liar, and the father of it.*

Heb 11:6 *But without faith it is impossible to please him: for he that cometh to God must believe that he is, and that he is a rewarder of them that diligently seek him.*

Ps 27:13 *I had fainted, unless I had believed to see the goodness of the Lord in the land of the living.*

1 Thess 4:15-18 *For this we say unto you by the word of the Lord, that we which are alive and remain unto the coming of the Lord shall not prevent them which are asleep. 16 For the Lord himself shall descend from heaven with a shout, with the voice of the archangel, and with the trump of God: and the dead in Christ shall rise first: 17 Then we which are alive and remain shall be caught up together with them in the clouds, to meet the Lord in the air: and so shall we ever be with the Lord. 18 Wherefore comfort one another with these words.*

Prov 24:10 *If thou faint in the day of adversity, thy strength is small.*

Mark 7:10-13 *For Moses said, Honour thy father and thy mother; and, Whoso curseth father or mother, let him die the death: 11 But ye say, If a man shall say to his father or mother, It is Corban, that is to say, a gift, by whatsoever thou mightest be profited by me; he shall be free. 12 And ye suffer him no more to do ought for his father or his mother; 13 Making the word of God of none effect through your tradition, which ye have delivered: and many such like things do ye.*

Matt 13:23 *But he that received seed into the good ground is he that heareth the word, and understandeth it; which also beareth fruit, and bringeth forth, some an hundredfold, some sixty, some thirty.*

Prov 4:7 *Wisdom is the principal thing; therefore get wisdom: and with all thy getting get understanding.*

Rom 9:6-9 *Not as though the word of God hath taken none effect. For they are not all Israel, which are of Israel:7 Neither, because they are the seed of Abraham, are they all children: but, In Isaac shall thy seed be called.8 That is, They which are the children of the flesh, these are not the children of God: but the children of the promise are counted for the seed.9 For this is the word of promise, At this time will I come, and Sara shall have a son.*

1 Cor 3:9 *For we are labourers together with God: ye are God's husbandry, ye are God's building.*

2 Thess 3:1 *Finally, brethren, pray for us, that the word of the Lord may have free course, and be glorified, even as it is wi*

Chapter VI

To Obey or Not to Obey

Whether or not we see the Word of God manifest in our lives is going to depend on whether or not we obey it. I believe that most people want to go to heaven and obeying God's Word is certainly the way to get there. But I often tell people that if their main motivation for living right is to go to heaven, they are going to have a hard life on this earth. Obeying God's Word not only ensures us a spot in heaven, but more importantly, obeying God's Word will allow us to walk in victory and manifest His will in the earth. Manifesting God's will in the earth not only take us to heaven, but it allows us to take someone to heaven with us. God's desire is that we obey Him in everything, but God knows that all that disobey do not do it intentionally. There are times in our lives that we do not obey the Word of God simply because we are ignorant of what the Word says. Years ago people used to say "What you don't know can't hurt you," but since then we have found that not to be true. Now we realize that what we don't know can kill us.

God knew when He gave Moses the law that the children of Israel would not keep it, which is why God gave them the system of the sacrifices. In Exodus Chapter 20, God gives Moses the law and then in verse 24

God begins to tell Moses about the sacrifices. God wanted the children of Israel to understand that if they sinned unintentionally, a sacrifice still had to be made. One might think, "Well I didn't mean to do it, I just made a mistake," and that may be true, but that doesn't stop the negative consequence. Have you ever heard that ignorance to the law is no excuse? That came from the bible.

Unintended sin still carries consequences. Even if we do things by mistake, we still set certain laws in motion that could hurt us. For example, if you are ignorant of the law of gravity that does not mean that the law of gravity does not work for you. If you stepped off of a building, you would still go down.

Num 15:29-31 *Ye shall have one law for him that sinneth through ignorance, both for him that is born among the children of Israel, and for the stranger that sojourneth among them.30 But the soul that doeth ought presumptuously, whether he be born in the land, or a stranger, the same reproacheth the Lord; and that soul shall be cut off from among his people.31 Because he hath despised the word of the Lord, and hath broken his commandment, that soul shall utterly be cut off; his iniquity shall be upon him.*

God, I wish I hadn't done . . . .

Every one of us, whether saint or sinner, has done things in our life that we wish we had not done and would like to go back and undo, but we can't. God has made a way for us to get our life right without going back and undoing anything, and it is called salvation. I know the church has for a long time preached and sang that salvation is free, but salvation is just free to us. Jesus paid a great price for it; He paid with His life. I remember as a child listening to my father preaching and he would say, "There's a price tag on sin." Sin was a debt that had to be paid for, but not by us. Through Christ we escape the death penalty of sin because of the blood of Jesus, but sin still carries temporary earthly consequences for the believer.

***Num 20:23-26** And the Lord spake unto Moses and Aaron in mount Hor, by the coast of the land of Edom, saying,24 Aaron shall be gathered unto his people: for he shall not enter into the land which I have given unto the children of Israel, because ye rebelled against my word at the water of Meribah.25 Take Aaron and Eleazar his son, and bring them up unto mount Hor: 26 And strip Aaron of his garments, and put them upon Eleazar his son: and Aaron shall be gathered unto his people, and shall die there.*

Moose had to suffer the consequences of his rebellion. Can you imagine how Aaron must have felt after all he had been through with the people? He would not be able to see the end results, the Promised Land. So for the believer, unintentional sin may not affect your relationship with God, but it certainly affects you earthly relationships with others.

One would think that a believer would not knowingly disobey God; after all He is God the Almighty, the Creator of all, the First and the Last. What believer in their right mind would not do what He said? I have sat and thought about it for hours trying to come up with a good reason that a believer would disobey God, except if he didn't believe God, but then he wouldn't be a believer.

Let's look at Balaam in Num. 22. Balaam was identified by God under the calling of a Prophet. This was a man that knew God and talked to God, a man that God talked to. Balaam even expressed his weakness before God; he knew that he could not do anything beyond what God said, but he still disobeyed.

Num 22:18-23 *And Balaam answered and said unto the servants of Balak, If Balak would give me his house full of silver and gold, I cannot go beyond the word of the Lord my God, to do less or more.19 Now therefore, I pray you, tarry ye also here this night, that I may know what the Lord will say unto me more.20 And God came unto Balaam at night, and said unto him, If the men come to call thee, rise up, and go with them; but yet the word which I shall say unto thee, that shalt thou do.21 And Balaam rose up in the morning, and saddled his ass, and went with the princes of Moab.22 And God's anger was kindled because he went: and the angel of the Lord stood in the way for an adversary against him. Now he was riding upon his ass, and his two servants were with him.23 And the ass saw the angel of the Lord standing in the way, and his sword drawn in his hand: and the ass turned aside out of the way, and went into the field: and Balaam smote the ass, to turn her into the way.*

Notice how God turned Balaam over to his own desires. God allowed Balaam to do what He already knew Balaam wanted to do. "Balaam's sin was so great that in Rev. 2, John refers to other sinners as "them that hold the doctrine of Balaam."

Rev 2:12-14 And to the angel of the church in Pergamos write; These things saith he which hath the sharp sword with two edges;13 I know thy works, and where thou dwellest, even where Satan's seat is: and thou holdest fast my name, and hast not denied my faith, even in those days wherein Antipas was my faithful martyr, who was slain among you, where Satan dwelleth.14 But I have a few things against thee, because thou hast there them that hold the doctrine of Balaam, who taught Balac to cast a stumblingblock before the children of Israel, to eat things sacrificed unto idols, and to commit fornication.

Do I really have to do what God said?

One attribute that God has that we don't hear much about is that God will not force us to do anything. I guess one could say that God is a real gentleman. This is one of the ways that man was created in the likeness of God: we have the ability to think, reason, and to make our own decisions. God will make a way for us, but it is up to us to walk in the way He has made. God will open doors for us, but it is up to us to walk through the door that He has opened. Many times in our lives we are waiting on God to do what He has already done and we don't realize it. Remember Moses at the Red Sea; he was asking God to do what God had already done:

Ex 14:15 And the Lord said unto Moses, Wherefore criest thou unto me? speak unto the children of Israel, that they go forward.

Notice how God responded to Moses: "Why cry out to me? Speak to the Israelites." Moses thought it was a time for prayer, but it was a time to get moving. When we pray we are talking to God, but we must remember that when we finish talking, then we must talk to our situation. Jesus tells us in Matt 21:21 to speak to the mountain:

Matt 21:21 *Jesus answered and said unto them, Verily I say unto you, If ye have faith, and doubt not, ye shall not only do this which is done to the fig tree, but also if ye shall say unto this mountain, Be thou removed, and be thou cast into the sea; it shall be done.*

God gives us all choices and He even tells us what to choose, but it is up to us to make the choice, and God will not do that for us. God's desire is for us to make good decisions and He makes it easy for us to know what is right. God does not hide His will from us; He wants us to have His will and do it. Would you tell someone about something that you had for them, and then hide it from them?

Deut 30:11-20 *For this commandment which I command thee this day, it is not hidden from thee, neither is it far off. 12 It is not in heaven, that thou shouldest say, Who shall go up for us to heaven, and bring it unto us, that we may hear it, and do it? 13 Neither is it beyond the sea, that thou shouldest say, Who shall go over the sea for us, and bring it unto us, that we may hear it, and do it? 14 But the word is very nigh unto thee, in thy mouth, and in thy heart, that thou mayest do it. 15 See, I have set before thee this day life and good, and death and evil; 16 In that I command thee this day to love the Lord thy God, to walk in his ways, and to keep his commandments and his statutes and his judgments, that thou mayest live and multiply: and the Lord thy God shall bless thee in the land whither* *thou goest to possess it.17 But if thine heart turn away, so that thou wilt not hear, but shalt be drawn away, and worship other gods, and serve them;18 I denounce unto you this day, that ye shall surely perish, and that ye shall not prolong your days upon the land, whither thou passest over Jordan to go to possess it.19 I call heaven and earth to record this day against you, that I have set before you life and death, blessing and cursing: therefore choose life, that both thou and thy seed may live:*

20 That thou mayest love the Lord thy God, and that thou mayest obey his voice, and that thou mayest cleave unto him: for he is thy life, and the length of thy days: that thou mayest dwell in the land which the Lord sware unto thy fathers, to Abraham, to Isaac, and to Jacob, to give them.

No, I don't want to

Not obeying God not only gets us in trouble in our everyday life, but more importantly, it gets us in trouble with God. I used to think that since God is God, and He can do all things, why doesn't He just make us obey Him? But I have come to realize that God knows that to truly obey, it must be done willfully, just like true love must be willful. This is why God must allow us to make our own choice, even if it is not the right choice to make. God compares disobeying to witchcraft. The English word witchcraft comes from the Hebrew word (*ƒsq*)), which is spelled *qecem* in English and pronounced keh'-sem, and means a *lot, or portion of divination (including its fee.)* We have learned that to obey God is to profit, so to disobey God is loss. Notice what God is saying: "*To disobey God and try to gain from it is just like witchcraft*". One important thing that this tells me is that God wants me to gain, but He wants to be the one that I gain through. Let's look at an example of this in scripture:

1 Sam 15:13-24 *And Samuel came to Saul: and Saul said unto him, Blessed be thou of the Lord: I have performed the commandment of the Lord.14 And Samuel said, What meaneth then this bleating of the sheep in mine ears, and the lowing of the oxen which I hear?15 And Saul said, They have brought them from the Amalekites: for the people spared the best of the sheep and of the oxen, to sacrifice unto the Lord thy God; and the rest we have utterly destroyed.*

16 Then Samuel said unto Saul, Stay, and I will tell thee what the Lord hath said to me this night. And he said unto him, Say on.17 And Samuel said, When thou wast little in thine own sight, wast thou not made the head of the tribes of Israel, and the Lord anointed thee king over Israel?18 And the Lord sent thee on a journey, and said, Go and utterly destroy the sinners the Amalekites, and fight against them until they be consumed.19 Wherefore then didst thou not obey the voice of the Lord, but didst fly upon the spoil, and didst evil in the sight of the Lord?20 And Saul said unto Samuel, Yea, I have obeyed the voice of the Lord, and have gone the way which the Lord sent me, and have brought Agag the king of Amalek, and have utterly destroyed the Amalekites.21 But the people took of the spoil, sheep and oxen, the chief of the things which should have been utterly destroyed, to sacrifice unto the Lord thy God in Gilgal.22 And Samuel said, Hath the Lord as great delight in burnt offerings and sacrifices, as in obeying the voice of the Lord? Behold, to obey is better than sacrifice, and to hearken than the fat of rams.23 For rebellion is as the sin of witchcraft, and stubbornness is as iniquity and idolatry. Because thou hast rejected the word of the Lord, he hath also rejected thee from being king.

Saul was God's first choice for the King of Israel, but Saul made some wrong choices and his choices cost him and his sons the kingship. Saul was trying to gain by disobeying God which means he was practicing "witchcraft".

In I Kings 13 there is a similar story. The Bible does not even give us the name of this man, but the Bible does say that he was a man of God. This man of God disobeyed God and it cost him his life.

1 Kings 13:21-24 And he cried unto the man of God that came from Judah, saying, Thus saith the Lord, Forasmuch as thou hast disobeyed the mouth of the Lord, and hast not kept the commandment which the Lord thy God commanded thee, 22 But camest back, and hast eaten bread and drunk water in the place, of the which the Lord did say to thee, Eat no bread, and drink no water; thy carcase shall not come unto the sepulchre of thy fathers.

23 And it came to pass, after he had eaten bread, and after he had drunk, that he saddled for him the ass, to wit, for the prophet whom he had brought back. 24 And when he was gone, a lion met him by the way, and slew him: and his carcase was cast in the way, and the ass stood by it, the lion also stood by the carcase.

I choose to obey

Choosing to obey is always the best way, by far. Unfortunately, most of us are old and have been through hell and high water before we figure that out. Just like there are negative consequences for disobeying God, there are positive consequences for obeying God. Obeying God should be the most important thing to a Christian. How we feel about it or what we think about it is irrelevant. Let's look at Simon in Luke 5. Simon did not think that Jesus had a good idea when He told him to launch out into the deep, and he even verbalized his opinion to Jesus. Simon obeyed Jesus, but he did not do it fully and with expectation. Jesus told Simon to cast out his nets. Simon cast just one net and it was old and rotten. If Simon had not had other ships around him to help, he wouldn't have gotten any fish even though it was God's will for him to have them.

Luke 5:4-7 Now when he had left speaking, he said unto Simon, Launch out into the deep, and let down your nets for a draught.5 And Simon answering said unto him, Master, we have toiled all the night, and have taken nothing: nevertheless at thy word I will let down the net.6 And when they had this done, they inclosed a great multitude of fishes: and their net brake.7 And they beckoned unto their partners, which were in the other ship, that they should come and help them. And they came, and filled both the ships, so that they began to sink.

Obeying God always pays off. Both the Old Testament and the New Testament teach this principle. Here are a few examples of how obeying God means success in life

Ps 119:9 Wherewithal shall a young man cleanse his way? by taking heed thereto according to thy word.

To obey God means protection

Ps 119:67 *Before I was afflicted I went astray: but now have I kept thy word.*

Luke 11:28 *But he said, Yea rather, blessed are they that hear the word of God, and keep it.*

Jesus has placed a blessing on anyone that obeys God. Remember, you are not blessed because you obey; you obey because you are blessed.

CHAPTER VI SCRIPTURES

Num 15:29-31*Ye shall have one law for him that sinneth through ignorance, both for him that is born among the children of Israel, and for the stranger that sojourneth among them.30 But the soul that doeth ought presumptuously, whether he be born in the land, or a stranger, the same reproacheth the Lord; and that soul shall be cut off from among his people.31 Because he hath despised the word of the Lord, and hath broken his commandment, that soul shall utterly be cut off; his iniquity shall be upon him.*

Num 20:23-26 *And the Lord spake unto Moses and Aaron in mount Hor, by the coast of the land of Edom, saying,24 Aaron shall be gathered unto his people: for he shall not enter into the land which I have given unto the children of Israel, because ye rebelled against my word at the water of Meribah.25 Take Aaron and Eleazar his son, and bring them up unto mount Hor: 26 And strip Aaron of his garments, and put them upon Eleazar his son: and Aaron shall be gathered unto his people, and shall die there.*

Num 22:18-23 *And Balaam answered and said unto the servants of Balak, If Balak would give me his house full of silver and gold, I cannot go beyond the word of the Lord my God, to do less or more.19 Now therefore, I pray you, tarry ye also here this night, that I may know what the Lord will say unto me more.20 And God came unto Balaam at night, and said unto him, If the men come to call thee, rise up, and go with them; but yet the word which I shall say unto thee, that shalt thou do.21 And Balaam rose up in the morning, and saddled his ass, and went with the princes of Moab.22 And God's anger was kindled because he went: and the angel of the Lord stood in the way for an adversary against him. Now he was riding upon his ass, and his two servants were with him.23 And the ass saw the angel of the Lord standing in the way, and his sword drawn in his hand: and the ass turned aside out of the way, and went into the field: and Balaam smote the ass, to turn her into the way.*

Rev 2:12-14 *And to the angel of the church in Pergamos write; These things saith he which hath the sharp sword with two edges;13 I know thy works, and where thou dwellest, even where Satan's seat is: and thou holdest fast my name, and hast not denied my faith, even in those days wherein Antipas was my faithful martyr, who was slain among you, where Satan dwelleth.14 But I have a few things against thee, because thou hast there them that hold the doctrine of Balaam, who taught Balac to* cast a stumblingblock before the children of Israel, to eat things sacrificed unto idols, and to commit fornication.

Ex 14:15 *And the Lord said unto Moses, Wherefore criest thou unto me? speak unto the children of Israel, that they go forward:*

Matt 21:21 *Jesus answered and said unto them, Verily I say unto you, If ye have faith, and doubt not, ye shall not only do this which is done to the fig tree, but also if ye shall say unto this mountain, Be thou removed, and be thou cast into the sea; it shall be done.*

Deut 30:11-20 *For this commandment which I command thee this day, it is not hidden from thee, neither is it far off.12 It is not in heaven, that thou shouldest say, Who shall go up for us to heaven, and bring it unto us, that we may hear it, and do it?13 Neither is it beyond the sea, that thou shouldest say, Who shall go over the sea for us, and bring it unto us, that we may hear it, and do it?14 But the word is very nigh unto thee, in thy mouth, and in thy heart, that thou mayest do it.15 See, I have set before thee this day life and good, and death and evil;16 In that I command thee this day to love the Lord thy God, to walk in his ways, and to keep his commandments and his statutes and his judgments, that thou mayest live and multiply: and the Lord thy God shall bless thee in the land whither thou goest to possess it.17 But if thine heart turn away, so that thou wilt not hear, but shalt be drawn away, and worship other gods, and serve them;18 I denounce unto you this day, that ye shall surely perish, and that ye shall not prolong your days upon the land, whither thou passest over Jordan to go to possess it.19 I call heaven and earth to record this day against you, that I have set before you life and death, blessing and cursing: therefore choose life, that both thou and thy seed may live:20 That thou mayest love the Lord thy God, and that thou mayest obey his voice, and that thou mayest cleave unto him: for he is thy life, and the length of thy days: that thou mayest dwell in the land which the Lord sware unto thy fathers, to Abraham, to Isaac, and to Jacob, to give them.*

1 Sam 15:13-24 *And Samuel came to Saul: and Saul said unto him, Blessed be thou of the Lord: I have performed the commandment of the Lord.14 And Samuel said, What meaneth then this bleating of the sheep in mine ears, and the lowing of the oxen which I hear?15 And Saul said, They have brought them from the Amalekites: for the people spared the best of the sheep and of the oxen, to sacrifice unto the Lord thy God; and the rest we have utterly destroyed.16 Then Samuel said unto Saul, Stay, and I will tell thee what the Lord hath said to me this night. And he said unto him, Say on.17 And Samuel said, When thou wast little in thine own sight, wast thou not made the head of the tribes of Israel, and the Lord anointed thee king over Israel?18 And the Lord sent thee on a journey, and said, Go and utterly destroy the sinners the Amalekites, and fight against them until they be consumed.19 Wherefore then didst thou not obey the voice of the Lord, but didst fly upon the spoil, and didst evil in the sight of the Lord?20 And Saul said unto Samuel, Yea, I have obeyed the* *voice of the Lord, and have gone the way which the Lord sent me, and have brought Agag the king of Amalek, and have utterly destroyed the Amalekites.21 But the people took of the spoil, sheep and oxen, the chief of the things which should have been utterly destroyed, to sacrifice unto the Lord thy God in Gilgal.22 And Samuel said, Hath the Lord as great delight in burnt offerings and sacrifices, as in obeying the voice of the Lord? Behold, to obey is better than sacrifice, and to hearken than the fat of rams.23 For rebellion is as the sin of witchcraft, and stubbornness is as iniquity and idolatry. Because thou hast rejected the word of the Lord, he hath also rejected thee from being king.*

1 Kings 13:21-24 *And he cried unto the man of God that came from Judah, saying, Thus saith the Lord, Forasmuch as thou hast disobeyed the mouth of the Lord, and hast not kept the commandment which the Lord thy God commanded thee,22 But camest back, and hast eaten bread and drunk water in the place, of the which the Lord did say to thee, Eat no bread, and drink no water; thy carcase shall not come unto the sepulchre of thy fathers.23 And it came to pass, after he had eaten bread, and after he had drunk, that he saddled for him the ass, to wit, for the prophet whom he had brought back.24 And when he was gone, a lion met him by the way, and slew him: and his carcase was cast in the way, and the ass stood by it, the lion also stood by the carcase.*

Luke 5:4-7 *Now when he had left speaking, he said unto Simon, Launch out into the deep, and let down your nets for a draught.5 And Simon answering said unto him, Master, we have toiled all the night, and have taken nothing: nevertheless at thy word I will let down the net.6 And when they had this done, they inclosed a great multitude of fishes: and their net brake. Luke7 And they beckoned unto their partners, which were in the other ship, that they should come and help them. And they came, and filled both the ships, so that they began to sink.*

KJV

Ps 119:9 *Wherewithal shall a young man cleanse his way? by taking heed thereto according to thy word*

Ps 119:67 *Before I was afflicted I went astray: but now have I kept thy word.*

Luke 11:28 *But he said, Yea rather, blessed are they that hear the word of God, and keep it.*

CHAPTER VII

LIVING BY THE WORD

How do we live by the Word? We live by the Word by allowing the Word of God to determine our choices and the decisions we make. Someone might say, "The Bible is old and outdated and not relevant to us today," but this is simply not true. As we study the Bible, we should not just look at the stories or the actions of the people in the bible, but we should look at the principles that the bible teaches us. Biblical principles are what we live by; this is why God left us His Word. Paul talks in I Cor. 10 about the behavior of the Children of Israel in the wilderness, but if their behavior was not good, why would we need to know about it? As examples for us about what not to do.

1 Cor 10:6 Now these things were our examples, to the intent we should not lust after evil things, as they also lusted.

I believe that as we study the bible we not only learn what to do, but just as importantly, we learn what not to do.

As I travel, teaching the Word of God, I find that the main reason given by young people for not studying the Word is that they feel that the

Word is boring and has no bearing on their life, which means that is how they feel about God. There is nothing farther from the truth. God gives us rules not to keep us from having a fun life, but so that we can have a more fun life. Notice what God tells the children of Israel in Deut 8:1. He says the reason He gave them the commandments is because when they followed them, they would live. This means that if they didn't follow them, they would die.

Deut 8:1-2 *All the commandments which I command thee this day shall ye observe to do, that ye may live, and multiply, and go in and possess the land which the Lord sware unto your fathers. 2 And thou shalt remember all the way which the Lord thy God led thee these forty years in the wilderness, to humble thee, and to prove thee, to know what was in thine heart, whether thou wouldest keep his commandments, or no.*

Many Christians find it hard to believe that God really wants them to have a good time and enjoy their life. Just ask yourself the question: do I want my children to have a good time and enjoy their life? You probably answered "yes". Now think—are you capable of showing more love and compassion than God? In order for us to live successfully by the Word, the one question that we must settle in our hearts is that God loves us and His plans are always for our good.

Jer 29:11 *For I know the thoughts that I think toward you, saith the Lord, thoughts of peace, and not of evil, to give you an expected end.*

There are times in our life that we have problems and we can't see any good end, but we have a promise from God. Having a promise from God is better than having a promise from any man. If a man promised you something, you would look forward to it and wait on it. So how much more should we look forward to the promises of God? We must remember that God sees the end from the beginning and He loves us, and if we hold on, we will see that God had us the whole time.

Rev 22:13 *I am Alpha and Omega, the beginning and the end, the first and the last.*

Matthew Chapter 4 teaches us that the Spirit of God led Jesus into the wilderness to be tempted of the devil. Jesus' confrontation with the devil was initiated by God! Jesus did not try to weasel out of the temptation; he knew that God was with Him and that the temptation would come to a good end for Him.

Matt 4:1-4 *Then was Jesus led up of the Spirit into the wilderness to be tempted of the devil. 2 And when he had fasted forty days and forty nights, he was afterward an hungred. 3 And when the tempter came to him, he said, If thou be the Son of God, command that these stones be made bread.4 But he answered and said, It is written, Man shall not live by bread alone, but by every word that proceedeth out of the mouth of God.*

Notice how Jesus fought Satan's temptation; He used the Word of God. Jesus just said what God had already said. This is the same thing we must do when we are confronted with temptation and unforeseen circumstances. We do not have to live as a slave to our circumstances or what the devil does to us, but we can live by the Word of God. We must learn to speak to our situation and call what we want.

Rom 4:17 . . . . *and calleth those things which be not as though they were.*

Note what the above text said: God *"calleth those things which be not."* Most of the time when we get in trouble, we talk about the trouble and we find that we are calling more trouble. But God said call what you don't have, the thing that *be not.*

Knowing the Word of God

Have you ever gone through a time in your life when it seemed like everybody had a word for you? Some of the words that you heard at that time were probably followed by, "Thus said the Lord." How do we know whether the words are from the Lord or not? Well the surest way to know is by the Bible. This is why we must learn to study the bible for principles. Principles teach us how to think. As a Christian, when we study the Word of God we can learn to have the mind of Christ.

1 Cor 2:16 *For who hath known the mind of the Lord, that he may instruct him? But we have the mind of Christ.*

God fully intended for us to fear and revere His Word, even when it came through man. God also knew that there would be false prophets and you can find them throughout the bible, both Old and New Testaments.

In Deut 18, God gave the judgment for false prophets, and He tells us how to recognize them. He also tells us not to fear false prophets.

Deut 18:20-22 *But the prophet, which shall presume to speak a word in my name, which I have not commanded him to speak, or that shall speak in the name of other gods, even that prophet shall die.21 And if thou say in thine heart, How shall we know the word which the Lord hath not spoken? 22 When a prophet speaketh in the name of the Lord, if the thing follow not, nor come to pass, that is the thing which the Lord hath not spoken, but the prophet'hath spoken it presumptuously: thou shalt not be afraid of him.*

Jer 23:21 *I have not sent these prophets, yet they ran: I have not spoken to them, yet they prophesied.*

False prophets are not just in the bible, they are upon us today. Anytime we speak and say God said and God did not say, we are misrepresenting Him, and we are walking in the way of the false prophet. There are people today that are not only misrepresenting God, but they are using the Word of God to do it, and God expects us to know the difference.

John 10:26-27 *But ye believe not, because ye are not of my sheep, as I said unto you. 27 My sheep hear my voice, and I know them, and they follow me:*

1 John 4:1 *Beloved, believe not every spirit, but try the spirits whether they are of God: because many false prophets are gone out into the world.*

How do we try the Spirit? We try the Spirit by the Spirit. If we encounter someone with a spirit that does not line up with the Spirit of God, then that spirit is not from God.

Man fulfills the Word of the lord

We know that nothing happens in the earth without God's knowledge, but we must realize that God's knowledge does not mean God's permission. Knowing that God knows everything that is going to happen is encouraging, but at times it can be frustrating, especially when something bad happens. God not only knows everything that is going to happen, He even tells us in the bible what is going to happen.

The main thing that Jesus taught in His earthly ministry is that we should believe. But what are we to believe? We are to believe the Word of God. Jesus knows that if we believe the Word, then we will know what is going to happen and we will be in a better position to do the will of God. Another side to knowing what is going to happen is that it will increase our prayer life. Eccl. 1:18 warns us that knowledge brings sorrows:

Eccl 1:18 For in much wisdom is much grief: and he that increaseth knowledge increaseth sorrow.

How can this be? You would think that the more you know, the better off you are, right? But this text says that the more you know, the more you have to be sorrowful about. So we see that being in the know is not always a good thing, but at times it can be. Can you imagine what your life would be like if you knew exactly what was going to happen in your life? This is how Jesus lived His life on the earth; He knew what was going to happen. Jesus knew what was going to happen when He prayed. Jesus knew what was going to happen when He called out a demon. Jesus knew when He blessed the bread that it would multiply. How did Jesus know that when He spoke things would happen? He knew by faith, the same faith that you and I should have.

One fascinating thing about knowing everything is that there are no surprises. Not ever being surprised is great for God, but as a man living in the earth, I don't think we would be happy with no surprises. Knowing that God is never surprised is really comforting, especially when we are going through something. It is good to know that God already knows that you are going to come out on top. God also knows what part each of us is going to play in bringing His will to pass in the earth. I believe that everything that happens to us as a child of God has a part to play in bringing God's will to pass in the earth.

In 1 Sam. 16; 1 God sent Samuel to anoint the new king of Israel, David

1 Sam 16:1 And the Lord said unto Samuel, How long wilt thou mourn for Saul, seeing I have rejected him from reigning over Israel? fill thine horn with oil, and go, I will send thee to Jesse the Bethlehemite: for I have provided me a king among his sons.

In 1 Sam. 16:13 Samuel anoints David who is just a boy at the time.

1 Sam 16:13 Then Samuel took the horn of oil, and anointed him in the midst of his brethren: and the Spirit of the Lord came upon David from that day forward. So Samuel rose up, and went to Ramah.

David went through a lot before he became king, even though he was anointed as a boy and had the Spirit of the Lord upon him from that day forward. In 1 Chron 11:3 we see the phrase *"they anointed David king over Israel"*

1 Chron 11:3 *Therefore came all the elders of Israel to the king to Hebron; and David made a covenant with them in Hebron before the Lord; and they anointed David king over Israel, according to the word of the Lord by Samuel.*

So when was David the king of Israel? When *"Samuel took the horn of oil, and anointed him"* in *1 Sam 16:13* or when *"they anointed"* him in *1 Chron 11:3*? We see this pattern throughout the Bible; God speaks and man carries out what God has spoken in His Word. Most of the time that we do God's will, we are not even aware of it. This is exactly how God brought about salvation through His son Jesus. Even though man placed Jesus on the cross, God had already spoken about it through the Old Testament prophets and the people were not even aware of what they were doing.

1 Cor 2:7-8 *But we speak the wisdom of God in a mystery, even the hidden wisdom, which God ordained before the world unto our glory: 8 Which none of the princes of this world knew: for had they known it, they would not have crucified the Lord of glory.*

Man seeks the Word of the lord

Man was created by the Word of God, and came from God: so it stands to reason that man needs the Word of God to survive. Whatever something has come from is what it needs to survive. As a Spirit-filled Christian we must understand that the Word of God is what feeds our spirit.

Matt 4:4 *But he answered and said, It is written, Man shall not live by bread alone, but by every word that proceedeth out of the mouth of God.*

Jesus did not deny that man lives by bread; He just denied that man lives by bread alone. Man's physical body lives by bread, but man's born-again spirit lives by the Word of God, because it is born of God, and whatever something has come from, that is what it needs to survive. Jesus used the term "needful" to describe the Word of God in Luke 10:42:

Luke 10:42 *But one thing is needful: and Mary hath chosen that good part, which shall not be taken away from her.*

We know that the Word is not needful for our flesh, but we can rest assured that it is needful to our spirit. God's Word is a sure thing, and how many sure things do you know of in the world?

Chapter VII Scriptures

1 Cor 10:6 *Now these things were our examples, to the intent we should not lust after evil things, as they also lusted.*

Deut 8:1-2 *All the commandments which I command thee this day shall ye observe to do, that ye may live, and multiply, and go in and possess the land which the Lord sware unto your fathers.2 And thou shalt remember all the way which the Lord thy God led thee these forty years in the wilderness, to humble thee, and to prove thee, to know what was in thine heart, whether thou wouldest keep his commandments, or no.*

Jer 29:11 *For I know the thoughts that I think toward you, saith the Lord, thoughts of peace, and not of evil, to give you an expected end.*

Rev 22:13 *I am Alpha and Omega, the beginning and the end, the first and the last.*

Matt 4:1-4*Then was Jesus led up of the Spirit into the wilderness to be tempted of the devil.2 And when he had fasted forty days and forty nights, he was afterward an hungred.3 And when the tempter came to him, he said, If thou be the Son of God, command that these stones be made bread.4 But he answered and said, It is written, Man shall not live by bread alone, but by every word that proceedeth out of the mouth of God.*

Rom 4:17 *(As it is written, I have made thee a father of many nations,) before him whom he believed, even God, who quickeneth the dead, and calleth those things which be not as though they were.*

1 Cor 2:16 *For who hath known the mind of the Lord, that he may instruct him? But we have the mind of Christ.*

Deut 18:20-22 *But the prophet, which shall presume to speak a word in my name, which I have not commanded him to speak, or that shall speak in the name of other gods, even that prophet shall die.21 And if thou say in thine heart, How shall we know the word which the Lord hath not spoken? 22 When a prophet speaketh in the name of the Lord, if the thing follow not, nor come to pass, that is the thing which the Lord hath not spoken, but the prophet hath spoken it presumptuously: thou shalt not be afraid of him.*

Jer 23:21 *I have not sent these prophets, yet they ran: I have not spoken to them, yet they prophesied.*

John 10:26-27*But ye believe not, because ye are not of my sheep, as I said unto you.27 My sheep hear my voice, and I know them, and they follow me:*

1 John 4:1 *Beloved, believe not every spirit, but try the spirits whether they are of God: because many false prophets are gone out into the world*

Eccl 1:18 *For in much wisdom is much grief: and he that increaseth knowledge increaseth sorrow.*

1 Sam 16:1 *And the Lord said unto Samuel, How long wilt thou mourn for Saul, seeing I have rejected him from reigning over Israel? fill thine horn with oil, and go, I will send thee to Jesse the Bethlehemite: for I have provided me a king among his sons.*

1 Sam 16:13 *Then Samuel took the horn of oil, and anointed him in the midst of his brethren: and the Spirit of the Lord came upon David from that day forward. So Samuel rose up, and went to Ramah.*

1 Cor 2:7-8 *But we speak the wisdom of God in a mystery, even the hidden wisdom, which God ordained before the world unto our glory:8 Which none of the princes of this world knew: for had they known it, they would not have crucified the Lord of glory.*

Matt 4:4 *But he answered and said, It is written, Man shall not live by bread alone, but by every word that proceedeth out of the mouth of God.*

Luke 10:42 *But one thing is needful: and Mary hath chosen that good part, which shall not be taken away from her.*

Chapter VIII

Watch your mouth

I can remember my dad saying to me, "Boy, you better watch your mouth." Throughout the scriptures we consistently see that our words play a large part in our life in the earth. God allows David to see this by revelation. David knew that watching his mouth on his own would be next to impossible so he prayed to God to give him help.

Ps 141:3 Set a watch, O Lord, before my mouth; keep the door of my lips.

David refers to his lips as a door, a door that opens and closes, and allows things to go in and out. David knew that what came through his door would go into his heart. David realized that to guard his heart meant to guard his mouth. We see this principle in Psalms 103:5

Ps 103:5 Who satisfieth thy mouth with good things; so that thy youth is renewed like the eagle's.

David is blessing God and giving God praise. David said the reason God gives his mouth "*good things*" to say is to renew his youth. Just from that verse alone we see that God is showing us the relationship between what comes out of the mouth and the renewing of the youth. The psalmist uses the term *"good things,"* but does not tell us what the good things were that God satisfied him with. Based on the content of the text and his use of the word mouth, we know he must be speaking of words. The second part of the text use the term *"youth is renewed,'* so we know he is speaking of strength. This principle goes against how we normally think we get strength. With the understanding of how words affect our life, we can also understand how important it is what we speak. Speaking God's Word is always the best way to go; you can't go wrong when you say what God said.

God confirms His Word

I have always been what some people would call a mouthy person. There have been a few times I have let my mouth get me in trouble. The thing that I love about the Word of God is that I can speak it and I don't have to worry about backing it up, because God backs up His own Word. With God's Word we get to talk big about it and God always confirms His Word.

Jesus gives us the great commission before He leaves the earth. In Mark 16:15 He tells us to *"preach the gospel to every creature"*; that is our part in the great commission. In Mark 16:16 Jesus tells us that there would be a response from the listener—they would *"believe"* or *"believe not"*—and that is the listener's part in the great commission. God plays the biggest part in the great commission in that He confirms His Word, which we find in Mark 16:20:

Mark 16:20 *And they went forth, and preached everywhere, the Lord working with them, and confirming the word with signs following. Amen.*

God is always going to do just what He says. That is what the bible is all about, the bible is God's Word to man. We find even in the Old Testament this process whereby God speaks to the prophet and the prophet speaks in the earth, and God performs His Word. The only thing that is unsure about the Word of God is when it will take place. Let's take a look at Lam. 2:17 and see how God's Word was fulfilled even hundreds of years after it was spoken:

Lam 2:17 *The Lord hath done that which he had devised; he hath fulfilled his word that he had commanded in the days of old: he hath thrown down, and hath not pitied: and he hath caused thine enemy to rejoice over thee, he hath set up the horn of thine adversaries.*

As Jeremiah looks at the people of Jerusalem being taken captive into Babylon, he writes the Book of Lamentations. Based on the content of the Book of Lamentations, Jeremiah was not at all surprised by what was happening, nor was he the least bit upset with God. Jeremiah understood that God was just performing His Word that was spoken. We can learn a great lesson from the Book of Lamentations and that is that when we disobey God's Word we can expect to see the down side of the Word, and when we obey God's Word we can expect to reap the benefits from the Word.

Jer 1:12 *Then said the Lord unto me, Thou hast well seen: for I will hasten my word to perform it.*

God reveals Himself by His word

1 Sam 3:21 *And the Lord appeared again in Shiloh: for the Lord revealed himself to Samuel in Shiloh by the word of the Lord.*

God reveals Himself by His Word. This is very important for us to remember, so we won't start thinking that God reveals Himself by our words. It is God's words that God responds to, not our words. As a Christian you should have the same agenda as God. Having the same agenda as God means you have the same priorities as God. As we study the Word of God, we should take on the mind of God. When we take on the mind of God, we begin to think like God, and see things the way God sees them. This is the whole reason I must renew my mind to God's way of thinking, so that I can see things the way God sees them. Once I begin to see things the way God sees them, then I can begin to speak the way God wants me to speak. If I think like God, I am going to speak like God. This is why God was able to reveal Himself to Samuel by His Word, because Samuel was speaking God's Word, or you could say Samuel was speaking the mind of God.

Just as it is critical that we speak God's Word, it is also critical that we understand God's Word. If we hear the Word without understanding, it is not going to do us any good. Look at what Paul said in Rom. 10:14:

Rom 10:14 *How then shall they call on him in whom they have not believed? and how shall they believe in him of whom they have not heard? and how shall they <u>hear</u> without a preacher?*

The word "hear" in the above text is used as a primary verb and comes from the Greek word "α'κου" and is pronounced 'akouo (ak-oo'-o).' It means *"to understand, perceive the sense of what is said"*. The reason God calls preachers and teachers is to give understanding to His Word. This is what Paul was talking about when he wrote to Timothy.

2 Tim 2:15 Study to shew thyself approved unto God, a workman that needeth not to be ashamed, rightly dividing the word of truth.

Hearing God's Word

As Christians we know how important hearing is. In fact, we get our faith by hearing.

Rom 10:17 So then faith cometh by hearing, and hearing by the word of God.

This verse sounds deep and spiritual, but there is nothing deep about it. If you were to really think about it you would realize that the more you hear something, the more likely you are to believe it. This is why God wants us to hear the Word of God. Notice the text said *"hearing"* not having heard, which means this is a continuing process.

I believe that God is always speaking; it is just that we have a problem hearing. Have you ever noticed how some people, even Christians, will look at you when you say something like "God told me"? Some Christians have never heard the voice of God, not because God is not speaking, but because they do not expect to hear His voice. To hear the voice of God we must receive it the same way that we receive anything from God, and that is by Faith. There are times that we may receive the Word of God in error. We must remember that while God's Word is perfect, we are imperfect beings, so we can perceive the Word in error. This is why confirmation is always good. If we are in sin it can also affect how we hear from God. Let's look at an example of this in scripture:

2 Sam 24:10-11 *And David's heart smote him after that he had numbered the people. And David said unto the Lord, I have sinned greatly in that I have done: and now, I beseech thee, O Lord, take away the iniquity of thy servant; for I have done very foolishly. 11 For when David was up in the morning, the word of the Lord came unto the prophet Gad, David's seer, saying,*

In verse 10 the text said that *"David's heart smote him after that he had numbered the people."* David acknowledged his sin and he recognized that he had iniquity in his heart, so he did not hear from God. God still loved David, and his promise to David was still in effect, but God chose to send His Word through the prophet Gad, probably to avoid error caused by David's inability to hear God properly.

God's Word will stand

We can always count on the Word of God. God's Word will come to pass whether we are around to see it or not. God made a promise to David concerning his seed. Now that David was about to die, he charged his son Solomon to keep the charge of the Lord his God, to walk in God's ways, so that he would prosper just as God had promised.

1 Kings 2:1-4 *Now the days of David drew nigh that he should die; and he charged Solomon his son, saying, 2 I go the way of all the earth: be thou strong therefore, and shew thyself a man; 3 And keep the charge of the Lord thy God, to walk in his ways, to keep his statutes, and his commandments, and his judgments, and his testimonies, as it is written in the law of Moses, that thou mayest prosper in all that thou doest, and whithersoever thou turnest thyself: 4 That the Lord may continue his word which he spake concerning me, saying, If thy children take heed to their way, to walk before me in truth with all their heart and with all their soul, there shall not fail thee (said he) a man on the throne of Israel.*

God confirms what He told David by telling Solomon the same thing. By this time David is dead, but God's Word is still good. This should encourage us to never stop praying and believing God. I can remember as a child I would lie in bed at night and listen to my dad downstairs praying for me. I did not give my life to God until my dad had been dead for eight years. Dad had died, but his faith was still working.

1 Kings 6:11-12 *And the word of the Lord came to Solomon, saying, 12 Concerning this house which thou art in building, if thou wilt walk in my statutes, and execute my judgments, and keep all my commandments to walk in them; then will I perform my word with thee, which I spake unto David thy father:*

There are times we all have to remind ourselves that we don't need to see the Word of God come to pass for it to be true. We must remember God's Word is true whether we see it come true or not. God warns us in

Mark 8:38 not to be ashamed of Him or His words. I believe one of the main reasons that we would be ashamed of God's Word is fear that what God said in His Word will not come to pass.

Mark 8:38 *Whosoever therefore shall be ashamed of me and of my words in this adulterous and sinful generation; of him also shall the Son of man be ashamed, when he cometh in the glory of his Father with the holy angels.*

Why do I need the Word of God?

Deut 8:3 *And he humbled thee, and suffered thee to hunger, and fed thee with manna, which thou knewest not, neither did thy fathers know; that he might make thee know that man doth not live by bread only, but by every word that proceedeth out of the mouth of the Lord doth man live.*

The Word of God is not optional, it is not up for debate; if we are to live, we can only do it by the Word. The Word of God is our lifeline; it is what we live by. Jesus makes reference to this text when He is tempted by Satan in the wilderness:

Matt 4:4 *But he answered and said, It is written, Man shall not live by bread alone, but by every word that proceedeth out of the mouth of God.*

To fully understand the meaning of what Jesus said we must understand that man is made up of Spirit, Soul, and Body. Yes, our body needs bread to live because it is physical, but our Spirit needs the Word of God to live because it is Spirit.

John 6:63 *It is the spirit that quickeneth; the flesh profiteth nothing: the words that I speak unto you, they are spirit, and they are life.*

To be strong in the Spirit, a Christian only needs to feast on the Word of God. Just like our physical bodies need bread to stay strong, our Spiritual bodies need the Word of God to stay strong. When you are faced with a temptation and your physical man wants to do the wrong thing and your spirit man wants to do the right thing, which man will win out? The strongest man will win, the one that gets the most nourishment.

Chapter VIII Scriptures

Ps 141:3 *Set a watch, O Lord, before my mouth; keep the door of my lips*

Ps 103:5 *Who satisfieth thy mouth with good things; so that thy youth is renewed like the eagle's.*

Mark 16:20 *And they went forth, and preached everywhere, the Lord working with them, and confirming the word with signs following. Amen.*

Lam 2:17 *The Lord hath done that which he had devised; he hath fulfilled his word that he had commanded in the days of old: he hath thrown down, and hath not pitied: and he hath caused thine enemy to rejoice over thee, he hath set up the horn of thine adversaries.*

Jer 1:12 *Then said the Lord unto me, Thou hast well seen: for I will hasten my word to perform it.*

1 Sam 3:21 *And the Lord appeared again in Shiloh: for the Lord revealed himself to Samuel in Shiloh by the word of the Lord.*

Rom 10:14 *How then shall they call on him in whom they have not believed? and how shall they believe in him of whom they have not heard? and how shall they <u>hear</u> without a preacher?*

2 Tim 2:15 *Study to shew thyself approved unto God, a workman that needeth not to be ashamed, rightly dividing the word of truth.*

Rom 10:17 *So then faith cometh by hearing, and hearing by the word of God.*

2 Sam 24:10-11 *And David's heart smote him after that he had numbered the people. And David said unto the Lord, I have sinned greatly in that I have done: and now, I beseech thee, O Lord, take away the iniquity of thy servant; for I have done very foolishly. 11 For when David was up in the morning, the word of the Lord came unto the prophet Gad, David's seer, saying,*

1 Kings 2:1-4 *Now the days of David drew nigh that he should die; and he charged Solomon his son, saying, 2 I go the way of all the earth: be thou strong therefore, and shew thyself a man; 3 And keep the charge of the Lord thy God, to walk in his ways, to keep his statutes, and his commandments, and his judgments, and his testimonies, as it is written in the law of Moses, that thou mayest prosper in all that thou doest, and whithersoever thou turnest thyself: 4 That the Lord may continue his word which he spake concerning me, saying, If thy children take heed to their way, to walk before* *me in truth with all their heart and with all their soul, there shall not fail thee (said he) a man on the throne of Israel.*

1 Kings 6:11-12 *And the word of the Lord came to Solomon, saying, 12 Concerning this house which thou art in building, if thou wilt walk in my statutes, and execute my judgments, and keep all my commandments to walk in them; then will I perform my word with thee, which I spake unto David thy father:*

Mark 8:38 *Whosoever therefore shall be ashamed of me and of my words in this adulterous and sinful generation; of him also shall the Son of man be ashamed, when he cometh in the glory of his Father with the holy angels.*

Deut 8:3 *And he humbled thee, and suffered thee to hunger, and fed thee with manna, which thou knewest not, neither did thy fathers know; that he might make thee know that man doth not live by bread only, but by every word that proceedeth out of the mouth of the Lord doth man live.*

Matt 4:4 *But he answered and said, It is written, Man shall not live by bread alone, but by every word that proceedeth out of the mouth of God.*

John 6:63 *It is the spirit that quickeneth; the flesh profiteth nothing: the words that I speak unto you, they are spirit, and they are life.*

Chapter IX

What shall we liken His Word to?

Isa 40:25 To whom then will ye liken me, or shall I be equal? saith the Holy One.

What can we compare God to? The answer is nothing, because He is in a class all by Himself. We will never fully understand God until we meet Him in heaven, but we can understand His Word and how His Word works. We must realize that God created us and He knows how He created our brains to work, and He knows what it takes to get us to understand His Word. We often use comparison as a way of understanding things. We compare what we don't understand to something similar that we do understand, thereby gaining some knowledge about the thing we don't understand. This process is called learning through comparison. This may sound difficult and confusing, but it is really quite simple, and is the goal of the parables in the bible. The process of learning through comparison is something we see throughout the bible.

The Word of God works like the rain

Isa 55:10-11 *For as the rain cometh down, and the snow from heaven, and returneth not thither, but watereth the earth, and maketh it bring forth and bud, that it may give seed to the sower, and bread to the eater:11 So shall my word be that goeth forth out of my mouth: it shall not return unto me void, but it shall accomplish that which I please, and it shall prosper in the thing whereto I sent it.*

I love the simplicity of the Word of God and in *Isa 55:9-11* God makes it even simpler. It is as though God is saying, *"You may not understand how my Word works, but I know you understand how rain works, and my Word works the same way."* Based on this text, the first thing we notice about the rain is that it comes from God. Rain is made by God and there is no substitution for it. We can also see that the rain comes from above, so man cannot take any credit for it. This is also true about God's Word.

Another interesting thing about rain is that it does not return to where it came from. Once rain comes to the earth, it is here and it is not going back up. When the rain comes down it will fall where God sends it; the rain does not pick and choose who it wants to fall on. The rain water's the whole earth and benefits all, the good people and the bad people. This is also true about God's Word. The rain makes the earth bring forth, and the earth does not have any say; the rain MAKES it bring forth what has already been placed in it. This is true with the Word of God. God's Word will cause things to manifest in our life that were there all the time. The Word of God will make what God has placed in us come forth.

Isa 55:10 said the purpose for the rain is: to *"give seed to the sower and bread to the eater."* Some people are sowers and some people are eaters, and whichever one we are, we need the rain. As with the Word of God, we can sow it into other's lives or we can just maintain our relationship with God. Whichever way we choose, we still need the Word of God. Without rain or water we would die, and so would the believer die spiritually without God's Word.

(***Matt 4:4 . . . ,*** *Man shall not live by bread alone, but by every word that proceedeth out of the mouth of God.)*

Without water, man can't make any of the things he makes. From the hardest man-made substance to the softest, one thing they all have in common is they all must have water added. God sends rain to the earth so that the earth can produce what God has already declared that it would produce. This is why we speak the Word over our lives and our children's lives, so that what God has already declared in our lives will come to pass. This helps me understand why my mother made me go to church, even when I told her I did not want to go. My mother knew that the Word would be spoken in the church and if she kept me in the "rain," whatever God placed in my life would come forth. This is why it is so important that we say what God has already said. This scripture, *Isa 55:10,* teach us how the Word of God works. His Words works just like the rain and I thank God for it, because we can't live without the rain or the Word.

Col 1:17 *And he is before all things, and by him all things consist.*

The Word of God works like a sword

Heb 4:12 *For the word of God is quick, and powerful, and sharper than any twoedged sword, piercing even to the dividing asunder of soul and spirit, and of the joints and marrow, and is a discerner of the thoughts and intents of the heart.*

When we think of a sword in this day and time, we usually think of a keepsake, or a decorative item that we hang on the wall and admire. In the time of the writing of the book of Hebrews, however, the sword was the supreme weapon of war, and in the hands of a skilled swordsman it became a deadly weapon. Not only was the sword a weapon, but it also had other uses. I can imagine that in the bible days, the sword was a very useful item. The sword was probably used for all types of jobs around the farm, as well as in war. The writer of Hebrews speaks of a two-edged sword, which means that the sword would work both ways. I believe that this is saying to us that the Word of God is very useful, and that it useful in more than just one way. The Word pierces, it divides. The text said *"dividing asunder of soul and spirit."* The division that the Word does is so important because it allows us to recognize what is of us and what is of God, what thoughts are coming out of our flesh, and what thoughts are coming out of our spirit. As Christians we must learn to weigh every thought against the Word of God.

Another thing we can learn from the sword is that, even with a sharp sword, the swordsman must be skilled in using it in order to win the battle. Likewise we know that the Word of God is true and right all by itself. With the Word of God being true and right, it still would be helpful for us to familiarize ourselves with the apologetics of our faith. Understanding why we believe what we believe will enable us to win people to Christ by explaining the Word of God to them. Note Proverbs 11:30:

Prov 11:30 *The fruit of the righteous is a tree of life; and he that winneth souls is wise.*

Knowing why we believe what we believe is a good thing, but even if we can't explain our faith, the Word of God is also *"a discerner of the thoughts and intents of the heart."* So if I am unable to articulate the Word with my mouth, I can always use my heart and live it out. This is why Prov. 11:30 says, *"The fruit of the righteous is a tree of life . . . .*

The Word of God is like a well of living water

The Word of God is not just like water, but living water. As we saw earlier, the water came from the sky and watered the ground. Water is also very useful to man out of the ground. We use the water for nourishment for our bodies; we use it to clean our bodies, and to wash many other things. The difference between water and living water is that living water is water that flows. Flowing water is usually fresher and cleaner. Jesus offers us living water.

John 4:13-14 *Jesus answered and said unto her, Whosoever drinketh of this water shall thirst again:14 But whosoever drinketh of the water that I shall give him shall never thirst; but the water that I shall give him shall be in him a well of water springing up into everlasting life.*

Jesus offered the women at the well water that would last forever. Jesus told the woman that the water would be in her a well of water springing up into everlasting life. The woman's resistance shows that she was thinking physically, while Jesus was speaking spiritually. Probably trying to be sarcastic, the woman said give me this water so I won't thirst again nor have to come to this well again to draw water. If you have ever drunk water from a spring, you know that it is always fresh because it is always moving. God's Word is always producing and bringing forth new things. Have you ever read a familiar scripture that you have read a hundred times, but now for the first time you understand it in a different light? That is the way God's Word produces understanding.

The Word of God is always springing up revelation after revelation. Not only do we use God's Word, but God also uses his Word. God uses His Word in several ways and for several purposes. God uses His Word to reveal Himself to us, and at times He will speak to us through His Word. God is always doing things all around us, but most of the time we miss it or can't see it. As we go to God's Word, we can communicate with God on a level that His Spirit allows us to understand. We can always visit God in His Word and we will always find Him there in His Word. We can always go to the Word of God and find comfort in troubled times. I thank God for the living water, the Word.

God's Word works like a plumbline

Amos 7:7-8 Thus he shewed me: and, behold, the Lord stood upon a wall made by a plumbline, with a plumbline in his hand. 8 And the Lord said unto me, Amos, what seest thou? And I said, A plumbline. Then said the Lord,

Behold, I will set a plumbline in the midst of my people Israel: I will not again pass by them any more:

A plumb line, as we know it, is a line that a carpenter might use in order to saw a straight line. A plumb line is also referred to by some people as a hook. Whether the plumb line is used to make a straight line or it is used as a hook it still descries the Word of God. As a hook God's word has the power to pull us or to draw us. Jesus teaches us in John 6:44 that we can't even come to the Father unless He draws us. A careful study of Amos 7:8 shows that both definitions would be appropriate. In Amos 7:8 God said ". . . . *Behold, I will set a plumbline in the midst of my people Israel: I will not again pass by them any more:*". The notion there is that God would not be there, but He would set them up guidelines to go by. That is exactly what the Word of God does; the Word gives us guidelines to measure our life by so that we will continue to please God. So even if we don't see God in our situation, we still have the Word as our guideline. This is why Paul tells us not to compare ourselves with ourselves.

2 Cor 10:12 *For we dare not make ourselves of the number, or compare ourselves with some that commend themselves: but they measuring themselves by themselves, and comparing themselves among themselves, are not wise.*

Many times people become offended by something that is said at the church, but if we use the Word of God as the plumb line and allow ourselves to be led by the Word, there is no reason to be upset with or offended by anyone. Too often we struggle in making a decision about whether we should or shouldn't do something. In some situations it is obvious what we should or shouldn't do, and then there are other times when we may need the plumb line. God's Word is our guideline, it keeps us going straight. We need to know what God said and what His opinion is about something because we certainly don't want to offend God.

God's Word works like a seed

1 Peter 1:23 Being born again, not of corruptible seed, but of incorruptible, by the Word of God, which liveth and abideth for ever.

It is almost impossible to try and describe the Word of God without using the word seed. God's Word is not only like a seed, many times in the bible God's Word is called a seed. In *I Peter 1:23*, Peter describes the new birth as being born of incorruptible seed. Being born of incorruptible seed means the seed will never fail; likewise God's Word will never fail. There are many mysterious and fascinating things about a seed. One of the most incredible things about a seed is that you always expect to get more out of the ground than you put in. Another fascinating thing about a seed is that, unless you have some knowledge about the seed, you won't be able to look at the seed and tell what it will produce. One would also have to have knowledge of how the seed worked and knowledge of the ground. The ground must be prepared before you put the seed in it, and the seed must be tended and cared for after it is planted.

Matt 13:3-8 And he spake many things unto them in parables, saying, Behold, a sower went forth to sow;4 And when he sowed, some seeds fell by

the way side, and the fowls came and devoured them up:5 Some fell upon
stony places, where they had not much earth: and forthwith they sprung
up, because they had no deepness of earth:6 And when the sun was up, they
were scorched; and because they had no root, they withered away.7 And
some fell among thorns; and the thorns sprung up, and choked them:8 But
other fell into good ground, and brought forth fruit, some an hundredfold,
some sixtyfold, some thirtyfold.

In the text above Jesus tells the parable of the sower. The one thing that I find fascinating about this sower is that he didn't seem to be too concerned about where the seed fell. After a careful study of the text, I noticed that Jesus referred to the man as a sower not a farmer. This man, being a sower, may have had limited knowledge of the seed and did not know how to get the most out of the seed that he had. This sower in Matt. 13: 3-8 seem to just throw seed anywhere in hopes that it will grow.

In Jesus' Sermon on the Mount, He taught that they should expect to get difference responses to the Word as they went out and preached the Gospel. In Matt. 6:7 Jesus tells them not to give what is holy to the dogs. This sounds to me like Jesus is saying that with some people you will just be wasting your time preaching to them.

Matt 7:6 *Give not that which is holy unto the dogs, neither cast ye your pearls*
before swine, lest they trample them under their feet, and turn again and
rend you.

As Christians we must learn to lead by the spirit of God in all things. We must realize that it is God's Word, not ours, and He knows where He wants it to be sown. We must also seek to become skillful in sowing the Word of God. We should learn to sow the seed that we expect to reap later and sow what we want to reap. I believe we must also look at where we are sowing and what attention we are giving to the ground after the seed is sown in it. God has given us the seed, which is His Word, so we have the ability to sow and reap. This is what God meant when He told Joshua that he could make his own way prosperous:

Josh 1:8 *This book of the law shall not depart out of thy mouth; but thou shalt meditate therein day and night, that thou mayest observe to do according to all that is written therein: for then thou shalt make thy way prosperous, and then thou shalt have good success.*

Please note that God never said that He would make Joshua a prosperous man. God said that Joshua could take His Word, or His law, and make his own way prosperous, and have good success. Too often we are praying for God to do what He has already done. God has given us the ability to make our own way prosperous and not only have success, but have good success. Thank you, Jesus!

The Word works like a fire

Prov 6:27-28 *Can a man take fire in his bosom, and his clothes not be burned?28 Can one go upon hot coals, and his feet not be burned?*

If you answered no to the above questions, you have all the knowledge you need about fire. It is almost impossible to come in contact with fire and not be changed in some way. Fire, like the Word of God, has no respect of person. Fire will burn anyone that comes in contact with it, it doesn't care who you are or how many days you fasted. Another interesting thing about fire is that no matter how small a fire is when it starts, it has the ability to quickly become huge and very dangerous.

Fire has many uses, especially in our homes. We can use fire to heat our homes, we can use fire for cooking at home, and we can use fire to burn our trash at home. The same fire that makes our lives so pleasant at home can also make us homeless. Fire, like the Word of God, can be used to work for us are against us. The word fire is used in the King James Bible 549 times. Fire is used in the bible to describe Hell, God, and the Holy Ghost. However we choose to use fire, it always demands attention.

Jer 23:29 Is not my word like as a fire? saith the Lord . . . .

CHAPTER IX SCRIPTURES

Isa 40:25 *To whom then will ye liken me, or shall I be equal? saith the Holy One.*

Isa 55:10-11 *For as the rain cometh down, and the snow from heaven, and returneth not thither, but watereth the earth, and maketh it bring forth and bud, that it may give seed to the sower, and bread to the eater:11 So shall my word be that goeth forth out of my mouth: it shall not return unto me void, but it shall accomplish that which I please, and it shall prosper in the thing whereto I sent it*

Matt 4:4 *But he answered and said, It is written, Man shall not live by bread alone, but by every word that proceedeth out of the mouth of God.*

Col 1:17And he is before all things, and by him all things consist.

Heb 4:12For the word of God is quick, and powerful, and sharper than any twoedged sword, piercing even to the dividing asunder of soul and spirit, and of the joints and marrow, and is a discerner of the thoughts and intents of the heart.

Prov 11:30 *The fruit of the righteous is a tree of life; and he that winneth souls is wise.*

John 4:13-14Jesus answered and said unto her, Whosoever drinketh of this water shall thirst again:14 But whosoever drinketh of the water that I shall give him shall never thirst; but the water that I shall give him shall be in him a well of water springing up into everlasting life.

Amos 7:7-8Thus he shewed me: and, behold, the Lord stood upon a wall made by a plumbline, with a plumbline in his hand.8 And the Lord said unto me, Amos, what seest thou? And I said, A plumbline. Then said the Lord, Behold, I will set a plumbline in the midst of my people Israel: I will not again pass by them any more

2 Cor 10:12 *For we dare not make ourselves of the number, or compare ourselves with some that commend themselves: but they measuring themselves by themselves, and comparing themselves among themselves, are not wise.*

1 Peter 1:23 *Being born again, not of corruptible seed, but of incorruptible, by the word of God, which liveth and abideth for ever.*

Matt 13:3-8 *And he spake many things unto them in parables, saying, Behold, a sower went forth to sow;4 And when he sowed, some seeds fell by the way side, and the fowls came and devoured them up:5 Some fell upon stony places, where they had not much earth: and forthwith they sprung up, because they had no deepness of earth:6 And when the sun was up, they were scorched; and because they had no root, they withered away.7 And some fell among thorns; and the thorns sprung up, and choked them:8*

But other fell into good ground, and brought forth fruit, some an hundredfold, some sixtyfold, some thirtyfold.

Matt 7:6 Give not that which is holy unto the dogs, neither cast ye your pearls before swine, lest they trample them under their feet, and turn again and rend you.

Josh 1:8 This book of the law shall not depart out of thy mouth; but thou shalt meditate therein day and night, that thou mayest observe to do according to all that is written therein: for then thou shalt make thy way prosperous, and then thou shalt have good success.

Prov 6:27-2827 Can a man take fire in his bosom, and his clothes not be burned?28 Can one go upon hot coals, and his feet not be burned?

Jer 23:29 Is not my word like as a fire? saith the Lord; and like a hammer that breaketh the rock in pieces?

CONCLUSION

GOD, MAY I USE YOUR WORDS PLEASE?!

Wouldn't it be nice if all we had to do was say what God said and it would come to pass? Have you ever noticed that in many cases in the bible, Jesus just spoke a word to people and they were healed? In Luke 13:12, Jesus told the woman *"Woman, thou art loosed . . . ."* Jesus did not touch her, He didn't lay hands on her, He didn't put in oil her. He just spoke a word to her. Jesus just told her that she was loosed from infirmity and she believed it.

Luke 13:12 *And when Jesus saw her, he called her to him, and said unto her, Woman, thou art loosed from thine infirmity.*

So why is it that when Jesus spoke the Word to people they were healed, but when we speak the same words nothing happens? What is the difference in what we say and what Jesus said? The difference is not in the Word, the difference is in the faith. We must remember the Word of God is the living word. The word is alive, it moves, it thinks, so it responds. But what does the Word respond to? Me? No, the Word responds to faith. We must get to a level of faith where we not only believe, but we know. We know that fire is hot; we don't have to test it, we don't have to think about it, we know it. Fire is not just hot some of the time; it is hot all of the time. Based on what we KNOW about fire, if we put our hand in it, we expect to be burned.

In this same way we know our name. If you were in an accident, the rescue workers would probably test your coherence by asking you something that they know that you should know, such as, "What is your name?" They know that if you are the slightest bit conscious, you should know your name. This is exactly the way we should use our faith. We must expect what we say to come to pass as if we know it will. Look at what Jesus told Nicodemus in John 3:11:

John 3:11 *Verily, verily, I say unto thee, We speak that we do know, and testify that we have seen; and ye receive not our witness.*

Jesus said He speaks what He knows, and this is what we must learn to do. But before we can know something, we must first believe it, and after we have experienced it, then we know it. The Word of God may be just words in the mouth of the unbeliever, but in the mouth of the believer, the Word of God is quick and powerful. If we want to see the Word of God working in our lives, we must believe what we say.

2 Cor 4:13 *We having the same spirit of faith, according as it is written, I believed, and therefore have I spoken; we also believe, and therefore speak;*

A good friend of mine often said it like this, "Say what you mean and mean what you say. If you can't say what you mean and mean what you say, then don't say nothing at all."

CONCLUSION SCRIPTURES

Luke 13:12 *And when Jesus saw her, he called her to him, and said unto her, Woman, thou art loosed from thine infirmity.*

John 3:11 *Verily, verily, I say unto thee, We speak that we do know, and testify that we have seen; and ye receive not our witness.*

2 Cor 4:13 *We having the same spirit of faith, according as it is written, I believed, and therefore have I spoken; we also believe, and therefore speak;*